LAS PUERTAS RETORCIDAS

(THE TWISTED DOORS)

An Educational Bilingual Mystery

LAS PUERTAS RETORCIDAS
(THE TWISTED DOORS)
Bilingual Spanish-English Edition

~~~~~~~~~~~~~~~~~~~~~~~~~~~~~~~~~~~~~

Whoever heard of curling up on a nice,
soft, warm couch to actually enjoy
learning Spanish?

The first chapters are a warm-up, but
you must learn them well *or else!*

Then, hang on tight to your pillow,
for this will be . . .

The Scariest Way in the World to Learn Spanish!

~~~~~~~~~~~~~~~~~~~~~~~~~~~~~~~~~~~~~

Written, Conceived, and Adapted by
Dr. Kathie Dior
Formerly of the Université de Paris

Spanish Translation by
Claudia Guerin, Ph.D. and
Cecilia Tenorio, M.A.

~~DIOR PUBLISHING~~

For bulk rate pricing, ordering, and inquiries:
call Dior Publishing at 1-877-622-3176; visit
our website at www.thetwisteddoors.com; or
email us at info@thetwisteddoors.com.

Graphics team: Krista Edmonds and Kathie Dior
Graphic artist: Krista Edmonds

Illustrations in chapters 4, 10, 13, 14, 29,
30, and 46 (figure 2) inspired by the original
Les portes tordues graphics: Andrew Edmonds

Audio CD direction: Kathie Dior
Audio CD narration: Nalda Baéz Smith
and Rosa-María Boisset-Brindle

A French version is also available:
Les portes tordues (The Twisted Doors):
The Scariest Way in the World to Learn French! ™
ISBN-13: 978-0-9710227-1-3
ISBN-10: 0-9710227-1-2

Las puertas retorcidas (The Twisted Doors):
The Scariest Way in the World to Learn Spanish! ™
ISBN-13: 978-0-9710227-2-0
ISBN-10: 0-9710227-2-0

Printed in the United States of America

~~ ÍNDICE DE CONTENIDOS ~~

I wish to dedicate this book to Stanley, Fay, François, Red, Bob, Ming, Gray, Beauty, Cookie, and little Abbott and Costello.

~~ ACKNOWLEDGMENTS ~~

I wish to express my deepest gratitude to Professor Servanne Woodward, the editor of the original French version, *Les portes tordues*, for her belief in me, without which, *The Twisted Doors* series would never have been written.

My sincere appreciation goes to the native Spanish-speaking translators of *The Twisted Doors* into Spanish, Claudia B. E. Guerin, Ph.D. and Cecilia Tenorio, M.A.

For their outstanding performance in revising this book for 2006, I wish to thank José Manuel García, La Universidad de los Andes, Bogotá, Colombia, M.A. in Teaching of Spanish from Purdue University, and Claudia G. Cervantes, Universidad Veracruzana, Veracruz, México.

Special thanks go to Pilar Marcé, Universidad Pompeu Fabra, Barcelona, Spain, M.A. in Teaching of Spanish from Purdue University and M.A. in Conference Interpretation, Monterey Institute of International Studies. Her expertise in revising the first edition of this book and her uplifting spirit greatly facilitated the work before us.

I would like to extend my special thanks to the graphic artist, Krista Edmonds of Edmonds Productions for her skill and rare collaborative effort and patience, and to Andrew Edmonds for his remarkable illustrations inspired by the graphics found in the first version of *Les portes tordues*.

Lastly, I wish to thank the Purdue University Gifted Education Resource Institute (GERI), West Lafayette, Indiana, for having faith in using *The Twisted Doors* series.

~~ PREFACIO ~~

This book and its accompanying audio CD are meant to take you on a most unfamiliar journey into the world of Spanish. Here are the directions for using the book itself: There are none . . . Well, maybe you need to know one thing: every line of the Spanish story will always correspond to the same number line of the English translation. For instance, look at Capítulo 1. Look at line 2 of the Spanish text. Now, logically speaking, which line of the English translation do you think will correspond to this line? If you said line 3, you had better send back this book! O.K. Those are the directions (or should I say "direction" with no "s" for the book). As for the audio CD, here are a few suggestions: Listen to it once as you follow the new Spanish text. Then go back to the book and concentrate on learning the chapter. When you have passed the chapter test, listen to the CD again with the book open and then with the book *closed!* How many words or phrases can you now understand without peeking at the text? One last suggestion for the CD: For a zany subtitled effect that will skyrocket your acquisition of Spanish intonation, listen to the CD as you follow the *English* text! Now, are you ready to begin? If so, just turn to page 1, pop in the audio CD, find a nice comfortable setting, sit down (unless you prefer standing), and start to read and listen. You will see how to proceed and what you are expected to do. One note: Don't skip anything. You'll see why later!

If you find yourself pulling out perfectly good hair because you don't understand something, feel free to email me at info@thetwisteddoors.com.

One word of caution for Capítulo 13 and on:

Keep all your lights on!

K.D.

ENTRE...

Yo veo esta casa vieja todos los días.
Es muy grande, con un aire misterioso.
En realidad, tengo miedo de ella.

I see this old house every day.
It is very big with a mysterious air.
In fact, I am afraid of it.

yo = I
esta casa = this house
es = it is
* ser = to be
grande = big
un = a (masculine)
ella = she or it (feminine)

You had better learn how to conjugate the present tense of
the verb **ser**. Something tells me you should do it now!
This is friendly advice from me to you.

ser = to be

yo soy = I am
tú eres = you are
usted es = you are
él es = he is; it is
ella es = she is; it is
nosotr**o**s somos = we are (masculine)
nosotr**a**s somos = we are (feminine)
ustedes son = you are
ellos son = they are (masculine)
ellas son = they are (feminine)

Ah! You noticed that there are three ways
to say **you**** in Spanish! Let's make this simple:
You use **tú** if you are talking to a friend or to a
family member (that's why it's called **famil**iar).
It is always singular.
You use **usted** if you are talking to
your teacher, doctor, or a stranger.
It is a sign of respect and politeness.
It is always singular.
You use **ustedes** if you are talking to more than
one person, whether they are familiar or not.
It is always plural.

Now, if you haven't learned the **to be** verb, don't
go on! Heed my warning and then take this test!

1. yo = _____
2. ser = _____
3. ustedes = _____
4. ellos son = _____
5. casa = _____
6. un = _____
7. tú = _____
8. he is = _____
9. she is = _____
10. I am = _____
11. we are = _____
12. they are = _____
13. you (singular and polite form) are = _____

Here are the answers:

1. I
2. to be
3. you (plural form)
4. they are
5. house
6. a (masculine)
7. you (singular and familiar form)
8. él es
9. ella es
10. yo soy
11. nosotros somos or nosotras somos
12. ellos son or ellas son
13. usted es

If you scored 10 out of 13, you are probably
going to be all right. If not, study and retake the test.
You'll see why later! Go to Capítulo 2 if you fared well!

* One asterisk indicates that the word or phrase is not in the Spanish text. But beware! You must learn it too!

** Two asterisks mean that there is an important footnote such as the following: There are actually other ways to say **you** in Spanish depending on the country! For instance in Spain, the familiar and plural form of **you** is **vosotros** (masculine) or **vosotras** (feminine). This form is used as the plural of **tú** and is not commonly used in the rest of the Spanish-speaking world. In certain countries of Latin America, the word **vos** is used in the place of **tú**.

Yo estoy ansiosa.
Yo decido ser una niña valiente.
Camino hacia la casa grande y misteriosa.
Tengo mucho miedo.

I am anxious.
I decide to be a courageous girl.
I walk toward the big and mysterious house.
I am very afraid.

yo estoy = I am
* estar = to be
una = a (feminine)
niña = girl
la = the (singular and feminine)
y = and
tengo or yo tengo = I have
* tener = to have
mucho = very (much); a lot of; much
miedo = fear
tengo miedo or yo tengo miedo = I am afraid (think: I have fear)

Did you notice that there are two ways to say **to be** in Spanish?
SER and **ESTAR!**
You usually use **ser** to describe a *permanent* state of people
or things. For instance, if you are an intelligent person,
you would say, « yo **soy** inteligente » because you
will *always* be an intelligent person (hopefully).
You usually use **estar** to describe a *temporary* state of people
or things. So if you are nervous because of an upcoming
exam, you would say, « yo **estoy** nerviosa » because you
are nervous now but will *not* be after the exam. Get it?

Now watch out! For your own good, learn to conjugate
the present tense of the other **to be** verb **estar**!

estar = to be

yo estoy = I am
tú estás = you are
usted está = you are
él está = he is; it is
ella está = she is; it is
nosotros estamos = we are (masculine)
nosotras estamos = we are (feminine)
ustedes están = you are
ellos están = they are (masculine)
ellas están = they are (feminine)

Try out this little test. Learn from it now!
It will all come in handy later. Believe me!

1. fear = _____
2. mucho = _____
3. la = _____
4. usted está = _____
5. una niña = _____
6. ellos están = _____
7. ellos son = _____
8. yo soy = _____
9. yo estoy = _____
10. you (singular and familiar) are = _____ or _____
11. you (plural) are = _____ or _____
12. él es = _____
13. nosotras estamos = _____
14. tú estás = _____
15. I am = _____ or _____
16. she is = _____ or _____
17. we are = _____ or _____
18. they are = _____ or _____

Now here are the answers:

1. miedo
2. very (much); a lot of; much
3. the
4. you are
5. a girl
6. they are
7. they are
8. I am
9. I am
10. tú eres or tú estás
11. ustedes son or ustedes están
12. he is
13. we are
14. you are
15. yo estoy or yo soy
16. ella está or ella es
17. nosotros estamos or nosotros somos
    or nosotras estamos or nosotras somos
18. ellos están or ellos son
    or ellas están or ellas son

If you missed more than 3, go back and take the test again.
When you have succeeded, you may proceed with
caution to Capítulo 3, if you dare!

Llego a la puerta grande.
Toco a la puerta dos veces. . .
Un hombre alto llega a la puerta.
Abre la puerta lentamente.
Miro a este hombre.
Él es alto y muy viejo.
Tiene pequeños ojos negros y una mirada maligna.

I arrive at the big door.
I knock at the door two times . . .
A tall man arrives at the door.
He opens the door slowly.
I look at this man.
He is tall and very old.
He has little black eyes and a wicked look.

llego or yo llego = I arrive
a = at; to
la puerta = the door
toco or yo toco = I knock
dos = two
un hombre = a man
miro or yo **mir**o = I look at
tiene or él tiene = he has
* tener = to have
una **mir**ada = a look (think: **mir**ror)

You'd better learn your numbers if you know what is good
for you! Friendly advice from me to you! It will pay off later!

uno = one
dos = two
tres = three
cuatro = four
cinco = five
seis = six
siete = seven
ocho = eight
nueve = nine
diez = ten

Ready for another twist?
I bet you have been wondering why you can say **yo miro** or just
miro for **I look at**. Well, that's because when the subject pronouns,
yo, tú, usted, él, ella, nosotros, nosotras, ustedes, ellos, and ellas
accompany the verb, you don't have to say them!** The trick is
to be sure to attach the right ending to this verb. That is
how you can distinguish if a person is saying **I look
at** or **you look at**, etc. So, it's all in the ending!
Next thought: When **do** you use the pronoun?
You use it to avoid ambiguity or to emphasize!
So if you want to emphasize *I* **look at**,
you would say, « **yo** miro ».

Now beware of the endings and learn
the present tense of the verb **tener**!

ten**er** = to have

yo teng**o** or teng**o** = I have
tú tien**es** or tien**es** = you have
usted tien**e** or tien**e** = you have
él tien**e** or tien**e** = he has; it has
ella tien**e** or tien**e** = she has; it has
nosotros tenem**os** or tenem**os** = we have (masculine)
nosotras tenem**os** or tenem**os** = we have (feminine)
ustedes tien**en** or tien**en** = you have
ellos tien**en** or tien**en** = they have (masculine)
ellas tien**en** or tien**en** = they have (feminine)

Time is running out! So take this test. If you missed more than 3, study and take the test again or you will regret it!

1. tengo = _____
2. un hombre = _____
3. usted tiene = _____
4. la puerta = _____
5. ellos tienen = _____
6. ellos son = _____
7. toco = _____
8. I have = _____
9. you (singular and familiar) have = _____
10. you (plural) are = _____
11. él tiene = _____
12. nosotras tenemos = _____
13. dos = _____
14. three = _____
15. she has = _____
16. cinco = _____
17. they have = _____
18. seis = _____

Here are the answers:

1. I have
2. a man
3. you have
4. the door
5. they have
6. they are
7. I knock
8. yo tengo
9. tú tienes
10. ustedes son or ustedes están
11. he has
12. we have
13. two
14. tres
15. ella tiene
16. five
17. ellos tienen or ellas tienen
18. six

If you fared well on the test, go on to Capítulo 4!

** The subject pronoun is often put in parentheses to show that it is not necessary to say. Example: (yo) miro

NOTAS

CAPÍTULO CUATRO 4

« ¿Qué quieres? », dice este hombre con un aire maligno.
« Soy una niña curiosa », digo con una voz temblorosa.
« ¿Quieres ver mi casa? ¡Entonces cuenta mis dedos! ».
Yo tengo miedo pero cuento: usted tiene un dedo, usted tiene dos dedos,

usted tiene_____dedos,
usted tiene_____dedos,
usted tiene_____dedos,
usted tiene_____dedos,
usted tiene_____dedos,
usted tiene_____dedos,
usted tiene_____dedos,
usted tiene_____dedos.

« What do you want? » says this man with a wicked air.
« I am a curious little girl, » I say with a trembling voice.
« Do you want to see my house? Then count my fingers! »
I am afraid, but I count: You have one finger. You have two fingers.

You have three fingers.
You have four fingers.
You have five fingers.
You have six fingers.
You have seven fingers.
You have eight fingers.
You have nine fingers.
You have ten fingers.

Can you finish counting the wicked man's
fingers? If not, you're not allowed to find out if the
little girl enters his house! Warning! You may go
on to Capítulo 5 only if you have succeeded!

« ¡Bien, estás contando mis diez dedos! », dice con una voz malvada.
« Tú eres una niña curiosa.
¿Quieres ver mi casa? ».
Él abre la puerta lentamente.
Yo tiemblo.

« Good, you are counting my ten fingers! » he says with an evil voice.
« You are a curious girl.
Do you want to see my house? »
He opens the door slowly.
I tremble.

estás contando or tú **estás** contando = you **are** counting
* contar = to count
dice or él dice = he says
con = with
una = a (feminine)
una **vo**z = a **vo**ice
malvada = evil; wicked (feminine)
¿quieres? = do you want?
ver = to see
él **abr**e = he opens
* **abr**ir = to open
lentamente = slowly

Are you ready to learn your first **-ir** verb, **abrir**?
This just means that the verb ends in the letters **ir**!
It's not too difficult. Just take the root of the verb,
in this case, **abr**, and add the appropriate ending.
These endings are the same for most **-ir** verbs.
These endings are shown in **bold** print.

abr**ir**** = to open

yo abr**o** = I open; I am opening; I do open
tú abr**es** = you open; you are opening; you do open
usted abr**e** = you open; you are opening; you do open
él abr**e** = he opens; he is opening; he does open
ella abr**e** = she opens; she is opening; she does open
nosotros abr**imos** = we open; we are opening; we do open
nosotras abr**imos** = we open; we are opening; we do open
ustedes abr**en** = you open; you are opening; you do open
ellos abr**en** = they open; they are opening; they do open
ellas abr**en** = they open; they are opening; they do open

So, the endings for **-ir** verbs are
-o, -es, -e, -imos, -en.
Notice that **usted**, **él**, and **ella** have the *same* ending.
In this case, they end with an **e**.
Ustedes, **ellos**, and **ellas** also share the same
ending, in this case, **en**.
Memorize this now if you know what is good for you!

Now take this test! Doing well on it will be
important later on, if you know what I mean!

1. con = _____
2. él abre = _____
3. lentamente = _____
4. we open = _____
5. una voz = _____
6. ver = _____
7. I open = _____
8. él dice = _____
9. una = _____
10. diez = _____
11. tú abres = _____
12. he opens = _____
13. they open = _____
14. you (plural) open = _____
15. yo abro = _____
16. you (singular, polite) open = _____

Here are the answers:

1. with
2. he opens
3. slowly
4. nosotras abrimos or nosotros abrimos
5. a voice
6. to see
7. yo abro
8. he says
9. a
10. ten
11. you open
12. él abre
13. ellos abren or ellas abren
14. ustedes abren
15. I open
16. usted abre

If you missed more than 3, then practice
and take the test over. Otherwise, go on
to Capítulo 6 to find out what happens
when the little girl enters the house!

** The verbs you have encountered so far all belong to the present tense or more
exactly the *present indicative tense*. This tense simply *indicates* that the action
is occurring at the *present time*. But beware of this tense's translation trap:
abro can mean not only **I open**, but also **I am opening** and **I do open**!

La casa es muy fea.
Veo muchas puertas de madera.
« ¿Cómo te llamas, mi pequeña? ».
« Me llamo Francisca », digo con una voz temblorosa.
« Tú estás en **mi** casa », dice el hombre viejo.
« ¡Tú te vas a quedar en mi casa para siempre! ».

The house is very ugly.
I see many wooden doors.
« What is your name, my little one? »
« My name is Francisca, » I say with a trembling voice.
*« You are in **my** house, » says the old man.*
« You are going to stay in my house forever! »

fea = ugly (feminine)
* feo = ugly (masculine)
muchas = many; a lot of (feminine)
* muchos = many; a lot of (masculine)
la madera = the wood
en = in
el = the (singular and masculine)
quedarse = to stay

It's always a good idea to learn how to say, **My name is** ___.
So do it now, if you know what's good for you! One little
complication: **llamar** means **to call** and **llamarse**
means **to call oneself**. These are *both*, however,
-ar verbs, so learn these new endings now!

llamarse** = to be named or to call *oneself*

yo *me* llam**o** = my name is or I call *myself*
tú *te* llam**as** = your name is or you call *yourself*
usted *se* llam**a** = your name is or you call *yourself*
él *se* llam**a** = his name is or he calls *himself*
ella *se* llam**a** = her name is or she calls *herself*
nosotros *nos* llam**amos** = our names are or we call *ourselves*
nosotras *nos* llam**amos** = our names are or we call *ourselves*
ustedes *se* llam**an** = your names are or you call *yourselves*
ellos *se* llam**an** = their names are or they call *themselves*
ellas *se* llam**an** = their names are or they call *themselves*

Don't get scared by all these words!
What you should be afraid of is not knowing
this chapter! So, take this test!

1. our names are = _____
2. ugly = _____
3. my name is = _____
4. en = _____
5. his name is = _____
6. el = _____
7. madera = _____
8. muchas = _____
9. your (singular, familiar) name is = _____
10. their names are = _____
11. your names are = _____
12. quedarse = _____

Here are the answers:

1. nosotros nos llamamos
2. feo or fea
3. yo me llamo
4. in
5. él se llama
6. the
7. wood
8. many; a lot of
9. tú te llamas
10. ellos se llaman or ellas se llaman
11. ustedes se llaman
12. to stay

If you missed more than 2, practice and take the test over. If you did well, you may proceed with caution to Capítulo 7!

** *Llamarse* is called a reflexive verb (a type of pronominal verb) because the action of the verb reflects back to the subject such as in **I call myself** or **he washes himself**. Notice that the subject and the object of the verb are actually the same person. Reflexive verbs are conjugated with reflexive pronouns. These reflexive pronouns are **me**, **te**, **se**, **nos**, and **se**. **Me** means myself. **Te** means yourself. **Se** can mean himself, herself, yourself, yourselves, themselves, oneself, or itself. **Nos** means ourselves.

NOTAS

La gran puerta se cierra detrás de mí con un ruido fuerte.
¡Halo la puerta muy fuerte pero no se mueve!
« ¡Señor, déjeme salir de esta casa! ».
« ¡No, mi pequeña Francisca, tú te vas
a quedar en mi casa para siempre! ».

The big door closes itself behind me with a loud noise.
I pull the door very hard but it does not move!
« Sir, let me leave this house! »
« No, my little Francisca, you are going
to stay in my house forever! »

la = the (feminine)
* el = the (masculine)
cerrar = to close
detrás de = behind
mí = me
un = a (masculine)
* una = a (feminine)
un ruido = a noise
halar (or *jalar) = to pull
moverse = to move
déjeme = let me
salir = to leave
mi = my (Don't confuse this with mí!)
para siempre = forever

Nouns are feminine or masculine and singular or plural.
The articles **the** (el, la, los, las) and **a** (un, una, unos, unas)
must agree with the noun.

el (not **él**!) is a masculine singular article.
Example: **el** ruido = **the** noise
But watch out! **el** also comes
before a *feminine* noun if it begins
with a stressed **a** or **ha**.
Example: **a**gua is a feminine noun.
el agua = the water

la is a feminine singular article.
Example: **la** casa = **the** house

los is a masculine plural article.
Example: **los** ruidos = **the** noises

las is a feminine plural article.
Example: **las** casas = **the** houses

un is a masculine singular article: **un** ruido = **a** noise
una is a feminine singular article: **una** casa = **a** house
unos is a masculine plural article: **unos** ruidos = **some** noises
unas is a feminine plural article: **unas** casas = **some** houses

Not too scared for two more complications?

de is a preposition that means **of**, **from**, **about**, etc.
But **de** + **el** (**of the**) contracts to a new word **del**

Example:

del (a contraction of **de** + **el**) ruido = **of the** noise

Last complication (Whew!)

a is a preposition that means **to**, **at**, etc.
But **a** + **el** (**to the**) contracts to a new word **al**

Example:

al (a contraction of **a** + **el**) ruido = **to the** noise

Now take this test.

1. a noise = _____
2. the noise = _____
3. of the noise = _____
4. to the noise = _____
5. some noises = _____
6. a house = _____
7. to the house = _____
8. some houses = _____
9. to the man = _____
10. of the man = _____
11. the houses = _____

Here are the answers:

1. un ruido
2. el ruido
3. del ruido
4. al ruido
5. unos ruidos
6. una casa
7. a la casa
8. unas casas
9. al hombre
10. del hombre
11. las casas

Now watch out!
There might be traps in the house if you use the
wrong el, la, los, las, un, una, unos, unas, del or al!
So study! When you have missed no more than 2,
you may proceed with caution to Capítulo 8!

¡Estoy sola en esta casa grande!
Tengo mucho miedo. ¡No puedo salir de la casa!
Grito: « Señor, yo soy solamente una niña.
¡Déjeme salir! ».
« ¡No, mi pequeña! ».
Él empieza a reír.
¡De pronto, desaparece de mi vista!
¿Es él un fantasma? Empiezo a temblar.

I am alone in this big house!
I am very afraid. I cannot get out of the house!
I scream, « Mister, I am only a little girl.
Let me leave! »
« No, my little one! »
He begins to laugh.
Suddenly, he disappears from sight!
Is he a ghost? I begin to tremble.

sola = alone (feminine)
* solo = alone (masculine)
no = no; not
puedo or yo puedo = I can
no puedo or yo **no** puedo = I can**not**
yo soy = I am
* yo **no** soy = I am **not**
solamente = only
déjeme = let me
salir = to leave; to get out
pequeña = little; little one (feminine)
empezar = to begin
reír = to laugh
de mi vista = from (my) sight
un **fant**asma = a ghost; a **phant**om

Have you noticed that putting **no** before the verb
means **not**? Try this test if you're not a fraidy cat!

1. yo puedo = _____
2. yo soy = _____
3. yo **no** soy = _____
4. yo **no** puedo = _____
5. I am = _____
6. I am not = _____
7. I can = _____
8. I cannot = _____
9. salir = _____
10. no = _____
11. de mi vista = _____
12. to laugh = _____
13. un fantasma = _____
14. déjeme = _____
15. to begin = _____
16. to leave = _____
17. a ghost = _____

Here are the answers:

1. I can
2. I am
3. I am not
4. I cannot
5. yo soy or yo estoy
6. yo no soy or yo no estoy
7. yo puedo
8. yo no puedo
9. to leave; to get out
10. no; not
11. from sight
12. reír
13. a ghost; a phantom
14. let me
15. empezar
16. salir
17. un fantasma

If you missed more than 3, take the test again – or else!
If you did well, go on to Capítulo 9.

Corro hacia una puerta de madera.
¡La golpeo muy fuerte! ¡Nada!
Pero veo escrito en la puerta: **TO HAVE**
¿Qué significa eso?
Comienzo a decir en voz alta:
tener = to have
yo tengo = I have
tú tienes = you have
usted tiene = you have
él tiene = he has
ella tiene = she has
¡Efectivamente, la puerta empieza a moverse!
Por lo tanto, continúo:
nosotros tenemos = we have
nosotras tenemos = we have
ustedes tienen = you have
ellos tienen = they have
ellas tienen = they have
La puerta se abre lentamente. . .

I run toward a wooden door.
I bang very hard! Nothing!
But I see written on the door: **TO HAVE**
What does that mean?
I begin to say in a loud voice:
to have = tener
I have = yo tengo
you have = tú tienes
you have = usted tiene
he has = él tiene
she has = ella tiene
Indeed, the door begins to move!
Therefore, I continue:
we have = nosotros tenemos
we have = nosotras tenemos
you have = ustedes tienen
they have = ellos tienen
they have = ellas tienen
The door opens slowly . . .

corro or yo corro = I run
hacia = toward(s); in the direction of
nada = nothing
pero = but
veo or yo veo = I see
escrito = written
decir = to say
en voz alta = in a loud voice; out loud
efectivamente = indeed (think: **effectiv**ely)
por lo tanto = therefore
lentamente = slowly

Now take this test and check out
the answers below.

1. I have = _____
2. ellos tienen = _____
3. ustedes tienen = _____
4. tú tienes = _____
5. she has = _____
6. he has = _____
7. you (plural) have = _____
8. they have = _____
9. we have = _____
10. yo tengo = _____
11. nosotros tenemos = _____
12. you (singular, familiar) have = _____
13. él tiene = _____
14. ella tiene = _____

Here are the answers:

1. yo tengo
2. they have
3. you have
4. you have
5. ella tiene
6. él tiene
7. ustedes tienen
8. ellos tienen or ellas tienen
9. nosotros tenemos or nosotras tenemos
10. I have
11. we have
12. tú tienes
13. he has
14. she has

Did you miss any?
If you did, study and take the test again.
BUT BEWARE:
The wooden door seems to only open itself
when it is given the correct answers . . . *hmm.* So
when you have scored a perfect, you may cautiously
proceed to Capítulo 10 if you want to find out
what is behind this very strange door!

¡Lo logré! La puerta se abre completamente. . .
De repente, oigo algo detrás de la puerta. ¡Pum!
Estoy tan asustada. ¡Mi corazón late muy rápido!
¿Qué es esto?
La habitación está oscura. Avanzo con mucho cuidado.
No puedo creer lo que veo.
¡Es un niño con un pirulí pegado a la cabeza!
« ¿Qué estás haciendo aquí? ».
« ¡He estado en esta casa vieja por
dos semanas y no puedo salir!
Y además, ¡la puerta me hizo caer y ahora
tengo un pirulí pegado a la cabeza! ».
El pequeño comienza a llorar muy fuerte.

I did it! The door opens (itself) completely . . .
Suddenly, I hear something behind the door. Bang!
I am so afraid. My heart is beating very fast!
What is this?
The room is dark. I move forward very carefully.
I cannot believe what I see.
It's a little boy with a lollipop stuck to his head!
« What are you doing here? »
« I have been in this old house for
two weeks, and I cannot get out!
And what's more, the door made me fall and now
I have a lollipop stuck to my head! »
The little one begins to cry very hard.

¡lo logré! = I did it!; I succeeded!
algo = something
tan = so
un **cor**azón = a heart (think: **cor**onary; **cor**e)
latir = to beat
¿qué es **esto**? = what is **this**?
* ¿qué es **eso**? = what is **that**?
* ¿qué **es**? = what **is it**?
una **habita**ción = a room (think: **habita**t)
oscura = dark (feminine)
con **cuidado** = **care**fully; with **care**
creer = to believe
es un niño = **it is** a boy
* **es** una puerta = **it is** a door
a = to; at
una semana = a week
además = moreover; besides; what's more
caer = to fall
ahora = now
pequeño = little; little one (masculine)
llorar = to cry; to weep

Try this little test if you dare! You will
surely need to know how to do this later,
if you know what I mean!

1. what is this? = _____
2. ¡lo logré! = _____
3. oscura = _____
4. ¿qué es eso? = _____
5. es un niño = _____
6. un corazón = _____
7. ¿qué es? = _____
8. it is a room = _____
9. llorar = _____
10. it is a girl = _____
11. la semana = _____
12. moreover = _____

Check out the answers to this test below.
If you missed more than one, study and
take the test again or you will be sorry!

1. ¿qué es esto?
2. I did it!; I succeeded!
3. dark
4. what is that?
5. it is a boy
6. a heart
7. what is it?
8. es una habitación
9. to cry
10. es una niña
11. the week
12. además

You may proceed to Capítulo 11 if you feel **very**
secure about knowing this chapter. But
beware! I hear the old man laughing
somewhere in the house!

« Tranquilízate », le digo al niño,
mientras halo muy fuerte del pirulí pegado a su pelo.
« ¿Cómo te llamas? », me dice el niño.
« Me llamo Francisca. ¿Cómo te llamas tú? ».
« Me llamo Enrique. ¡Ay! ¡Eso me duele! ».
De pronto, vemos que la puerta se mueve.
Yo grito: « ¡Rápido, tenemos que salir de esta habitación ahora! ».
Mientras halo del pirulí aún pegado al
pelo de Enrique, corremos por los grandes pasillos
de esta casa vieja y fea.
Pero es demasiado tarde, ¡porque el viejo nos está persiguiendo!

« Calm down, » I say to the little boy
while I pull very hard on the lollipop stuck to his hair.
« What is your name? » the little boy says to me.
« My name is Francisca. What is your name? »
« My name is Enrique. Ouch! That hurts! »
Suddenly, we see that the door moves.
I cry out, « Quickly, we have to leave this room now! »
As I pull on the lollipop still stuck to
Enrique's hair, we run down the big corridors
of this old and ugly house.
But it is too late because the old man is chasing us!

le = him; her; you (singular, polite)
al (a + el) = to the
mientras = while; as
pirulí (or *chupete; *piruleta; *paleta) = lollipop
pegado = stuck (masculine)
el pelo = (the) hair
¡ay! = ouch!
eso = that
eso **me** duele = that hurts (**me**)
* doler = to hurt
de pronto = suddenly
tenemos que = we have to
corremos or nosotros corremos = we run
* correr = to run
el pasillo = the corridor; the hall(way) (U.S.)
vieja = old (feminine); old lady
demasiado = too
tarde = late (think: **tard**y)
viejo = old (masculine); old man
perseguir = to **purs**ue; to chase

Now here is your first regular **-er** verb.
Pay attention to the endings in **bold**. Many
-er verbs have these same endings!

corr**er** = to run

yo corr**o** = I run; I am running; I do run
tú corr**es** = you run; you are running; you do run
usted corr**e** = you run; you are running; you do run
él, ella corr**e** = he, she, it runs; he is running; he does run
nosotros, nosotras corr**emos** = we run; we are running; we do run
ustedes corr**en** = you run; you are running; you do run
ellos, ellas corr**en** = they run; they are running; they do run

So the endings for regular **-er** verbs are
-o, -es, -e, -emos, -en.
Got it?

Now take this test and check
your answers below.

1. we have to = _____
2. the hair = _____
3. el pasillo = _____
4. nosotros corremos = _____
5. I run = _____
6. tú corres = _____
7. you (plural) run = _____
8. yo corro = _____
9. they run = _____
10. we run = _____
11. I run = _____
12. you (singular, polite) run = _____
13. he runs = _____
14. ustedes corren = _____
15. él corre = _____
16. ellos corren = _____
17. viejo = _____

Here are the answers. If you missed more
than one, study and take the test again.

1. tenemos que
2. el pelo
3. the corridor; the (hall)way
4. we run
5. yo corro
6. you run
7. ustedes corren
8. I run
9. ellos corren or ellas corren
10. nosotros corremos or nosotras corremos
11. yo corro
12. usted corre
13. él corre
14. you run
15. he runs
16. they run
17. old; old man

Did you do well? If so, you may go on to
Capítulo 12. But watch out! The old man is
running after Francisca and Enrique in the halls!

NOTAS

« ¡Ah, allí están, niños! ».

« ¡Rápido, Enrique, veo una puerta de madera! ».

Pero en esta puerta vemos escrito:

LOS COLORES

« ¡Yo no me sé los colores! ».

« Yo tampoco ».

Pero, como el viejo está justo detrás de nosotros,

empujamos esta puerta de madera muy fuerte.

¡Funciona! ¡La puerta se abre!

Pero, ¿qué vemos detrás de esta puerta?

¡Un agujero grande y negro!

¡Caramba! ¿Qué significa este agujero?

Vamos a averiguarlo. . .

De pronto, estamos

cayendo en este agujero grande y negro.

« ¡Ahhhhh! ».

Mientras caemos, oímos una voz diabólica:

**« ¡Si empujan para abrir una puerta de madera
que exige los colores,
sin duda éstas serán sus últimas horas! ».**

« Ah, you are there, children! »
« Quick, Enrique, I see a wooden door! »
But on this door we see written:

THE COLORS

« I don't know the colors! »
« Me neither. »
But since the old man is just behind us,
we push on this wooden door very hard.
It works! The door opens!
But what do we see behind this door?

A big black hole!

Good gracious! What is this hole?
We are going to find out . . .
Suddenly, we are
falling in this big black hole.
« Ahhhhh! »
As we are falling, we hear a diabolical voice:

« If you push open a wooden door that demands the colors, surely these will be your last hours! »

allí = there
niños = children
* un niño = a child; a (little) boy
* una niña = a child; a (little) girl
vemos or nosotros vemos = we see
escrito = written
* escribir = to write
yo tampoco = me neither
como = since (Watch out! *Cómo* means *how.*)
qué = what (Watch out! *Que* means *that.*)
un agujero = a hole
vamos a or nosotros vamos a = we are going to
estamos cayendo = **we are** falling (gerund form)
* caer = to fall
si = if
sin duda = surely; without doubt
última = last (feminine)

Try another **-ir** verb if you dare. Do you
remember the endings to most **-ir** verbs?
Say them aloud! Did you say:
-o, -es, -e, -imos, -en?
If you don't want big problems later on,
learn to conjugate this **-ir** verb.

escrib**ir** = to write

yo escrib**o** = I write; I am writing; I do write
tú escrib**es** = you write; you are writing; you do write
usted escrib**e** = you write; you are writing; you do write
él, ella escrib**e** = he, she, it writes; he is writing; he does write
nosotros, nosotras escrib**imos** = we write; we are writing; we do write
ustedes escrib**en** = you write; you are writing; you do write
ellos, ellas escrib**en** = they write; they are writing; they do write

You have seen in this chapter that **estamos cayendo** means
we are falling. This tense is called the present progressive because it
emphasizes a continuing action in the present. Ca**yendo** (fall**ing**) is called
the gerund or present participle. In order to form this tense, all you do is
conjugate the present tense of **estar** and then add the present participle.
So, here are the rules for forming the present participle:

For **-ar** verbs, replace the **-ar** ending of the infinitive (trat**ar**) with **ando**.
So, the present participle is trat**ando**.
Example: she is try**ing** to see = ella está trat**ando** de ver

For **-er** verbs, replace the **-er** ending of the infinitive (corr**er**) with **iendo**.
So, the present participle is corr**iendo**.
Example: I am runn**ing** = yo estoy corr**iendo**

For **-ir** verbs, replace the **-ir** ending of the infinitive (abr**ir**) with **iendo**.
So, the present participle is abr**iendo**.
Example: we are open**ing** = nosotros estamos abr**iendo**

One little complication: For some verbs such as **caer** (to fall),
the **-yendo** ending is used instead to prevent awkward spellings.
So, the present participle of ca**er** is ca**yendo**.
Example: we are falling = estamos ca**yendo**

Now if you want to find out what happens to
Francisca and Enrique after this huge fall, take this test.

1. we write = _____
2. you (singular, familiar) write = _____
3. a child = _____
4. yo tampoco = _____
5. to fall = _____
6. estás cayendo = _____
7. él escribe = _____
8. they write = _____
9. usted escribe = _____
10. I write = _____

Here are the answers. If you missed more
than one, study and take the test again
or you will pay!

1. nosotros escribimos or nosotras escribimos
2. tú escribes
3. un niño or una niña
4. me neither
5. caer
6. you are falling
7. he writes
8. ellos escriben or ellas escriben
9. you write
10. yo escribo

Very uncertain circumstances now await Francisca and Enrique
because they forced open a wooden door without correctly
reciting **LOS COLORES**. Dare you proceed to Capítulo 13
to learn about the consequences of their terrible lapse?

Grito: « ¡Ay! ».
« ¡Ay! », dice Enrique.
« Me lastimé el trasero ».
« Yo también ».
« ¿Dónde estamos? », dice Enrique.
Miramos bien la habitación.
Está totalmente vacía, excepto por una pintura al óleo colgada en la pared.
« Enrique, esta pintura es muy extraña, mírala bien ».

I shout, « Ouch! »
« Ouch! » says Enrique.
« I hurt myself on my derriere. »
« Me too. »
« Where are we? » says Enrique.
We take a good look at the room.
It is totally empty except for an oil painting hung on the wall.
« Enrique, this painting is very bizarre, look at it well. »

me lastimé = I hurt myself
yo también = me too
también = too; also
¿**dónde** estamos? = **where** are we?
mirar = to look (at)
vacía = empty (feminine)(think: **vac**ant)
por = for
una **pint**ura al óleo = an oil **paint**ing
óleo = oil
colgar = to hang
una pared = a wall
bien = well

Do you remember the endings to **-ar**
verbs? You should! Here are the endings:
-o, **-as**, **-a**, **-amos**, **-an**
Say this aloud!

Now see if you can figure out for yourself
how to conjugate the following verb:

mir**ar** = to look (at)

yo _____
tú _____
usted _____
él, ella _____
nosotros, nosotras _____
ustedes _____
ellos, ellas _____

Here is the correct conjugation.

yo mir**o** = I look; I am looking; I do look
tú mir**as** = you look; you are looking; you do look
usted mir**a** = you look; you are looking; you do look
él, ella mir**a** = he, she, it looks; he is looking; he does look
nosotros, nosotras mir**amos** = we look; we are looking; we do look
ustedes mir**an** = you look; you are looking; you do look
ellos, ellas mir**an** = they look; they are looking; they do look

If you want to see what is so bizarre about
the painting on the wall, you may go on
to Capítulo 14. But make sure you know
how to conjugate **-ar** verbs first or else!

CAPÍTULO CATORCE 14

Miramos con cuidado la pintura al óleo.
Vemos algo muy extraño.
¡En efecto, la pintura parece estar **viva**!
En la pintura vemos a un niño vestido de rojo y
azul que está tratando de abrir unas puertas de madera.
Pero estas puertas no son comunes.
¡Están *retorcidas*!
Sin embargo, ésta no es la única cosa extraña:
¡el pequeño de la pintura es igual a Enrique!

We look carefully at the oil painting.
We see something very bizarre.
*Indeed, the painting seems to be **alive**!*
In the painting we see a little boy dressed in red and
blue who is trying to open some wooden doors.
But these doors are not ordinary.
*They are **twisted**!*
However, this is not the only thing bizarre:
the little one in the painting looks just like Enrique!

extraño = strange; bizarre (masculine)
en efecto = indeed
estar viva = to be alive (feminine)
vestido = dressed (masculine)
* el vestido = the dress
él está trat**ando** de abrir = he is try**ing** to open (gerund form)
* tratar de = to try to
no **son** = they **are** not (from the **to be** verb **ser!**)
retorcida = twisted (feminine)
sin embargo = however; nevertheless; yet
única = only (feminine) (think: **uniq**ue)
la cosa = the thing
igual = the same; equal (masculine or feminine)

In the mood to learn your colors?
Remember what happened to Francisca and Enrique
when they didn't know their colors? They fell
into a huge hole! So, here is your chance.
Take advantage of it.

rojo = red
amarillo = yellow
azul = blue
anaranjado or naranja = orange
blanco = white
negro = black
verde = green

This time you are not going to go on to
the next chapter without a test! So, take
this test if you want to find out about
the very strange live painting!

1. blanco = _____
2. to be alive (masculine) = _____
3. en efecto = _____
4. to open = _____
5. yellow = _____
6. negro = _____
7. green = _____
8. blue = _____
9. anaranjado = _____
10. equal = _____
11. red = _____
12. she is trying to open (gerund form) = _____

Here are the answers:

1. white
2. estar vivo
3. indeed
4. abrir
5. amarillo
6. black
7. verde
8. azul
9. orange
10. igual
11. rojo
12. ella está tratando de abrir

If you missed no more than 2,
you may proceed to Capítulo 15 to
find out more about this live painting!

NOTAS

« Enrique, ¿cómo es que esta pintura está viva?
Además, ¿cómo es que tú estás dentro de ella?
Me dices que has estado en esta casa por
dos semanas. ¿Estás seguro de eso? ».
La cara de Enrique palidece. Unas lágrimas
corren silenciosamente por sus pequeñas y lindas mejillas.
Pero, especialmente, los ojos de Enrique
están llenos de horror.

« Enrique, how is it that this painting is alive?
What's more, how come you are inside it?
You tell me that you have been in this house for
two weeks. Are you sure of that? »
Enrique's face turns pale. Tears
run silently along his little cute cheeks.
But especially, Enrique's eyes
are filled with horror.

¿cómo. . . ? = how . . . ?
¿cómo es **que**. . . ? = how is it **that** . . . ?; how come . . . ?
* qu**é** = what
dentro (de) = inside
una semana = a week
seguro = sure
eso = that
la cara = the face
palidecer = to (turn) pale (think: **pallid**)
las lágrimas = the tears
correr = to run; to flow
por = along; for
sus = his (plural)
linda = cute (feminine)
la mejilla = the cheek
llenar = to fill

Are you brave enough to sift through **this** and its plural **these**,
and **that** and its plural **those**?

Let's start with **ésta** and **esta** as examples since they look so much alike!
(And don't get confused with the word está from the **to be** verb **estar**!)

There are a few tricks to remember:

The *accent* over the **é** means it's a *pronoun.*
Example: me gusta **ésta** = I like **this one**
So, **é**sta, a pronoun, can therefore be translated as **this one**.
Also: me gusta **ésa** = I like **that one**

No accent means it's an *adjective.*
Example: veo **esta** casa vieja = I see **this** old house
So, **e**sta is an adjective.
Also: veo **esa** casa vieja = I see **that** old house

Second trick:

If it has a **t**, it means **this** or its plural, **these**.
If it doesn't have a **t**, it means **that** or its plural, **those**.
Look at the examples above and below.

Third trick:

If it's masculine singular, it ends in **e**.
ést**e**; est**e**; és**e**; es**e** = this one; this; that one; that

If it's feminine singular, it ends in **a**.
ést**a**; est**a**; és**a**; es**a** = this one; this; that one; that

If it's masculine plural, it ends in **os**.
ést**os**; est**os**; és**os**; es**os** = these (ones); these; those (ones); those

If it's feminine plural, it ends in **as**.
ést**as**; est**as**; és**as**; es**as** = these (ones); these; those (ones); those

Ready for another **this** and **that** complication?

Besides feminine and masculine gender,
there is a *neutral* form in Spanish!

Esto and **eso** are the neutral forms
(neither feminine nor masculine gender) of **this** and **that**.

Esto and **eso** are both *always* pronouns
(no, the accent rule doesn't work here, but the **t** trick does!)
and are used when the gender is not implicated.
They usually refer to a concept or to an object.

Example:
¿qué es **eso**? = what is **that**?
¿qué es **esto**? = what is **this**?
¿qué significa **eso**? = what does **that** mean?
¿estás seguro de **eso**? = are you sure of **that**?
esto es una puerta = **this** is a door
eso es un pirulí = **that** is a lollipop

So, this wraps it up for this and that! Now, do
you think you have the nerve to take this test?

1. that one (masculine)
2. this one (feminine)
3. these ones (feminine)
4. those ones (masculine)
5. Is **esa** an adjective or pronoun?
6. What is the masculine singular *adjective* for **that**?
7. What is the feminine plural *adjective* for **those**?

Here are the answers:

1. ése
2. ésta
3. éstas
4. ésos
5. adjective
6. ese
7. esas

Now, how about something simple?
You have surely noticed that questions are surrounded by a pair of
marks that look like this: **¿** and **?**. The inverted question mark is a way to
let the reader know that the sentence or phrase to follow is a question. This can
be very useful when it is not apparent if the concerned phrase or sentence is a
statement or a question. Look at this example: *(tú) eres un niño* = you are a boy.
If you were to turn this into a question, you would still say, *(tú) eres un niño*. In
spoken Spanish, you would indicate that this is a question by the intonation of
your voice, but in written Spanish, there is no way to designate this.
Well, yes there is: the inverted question mark! Problem solved.

Now, if you want to learn the incredible mystery that
is to follow, you had better do well on this test or else!

1. estás seguro = _____
2. ¿estás seguro? = _____
3. eso es una cara = _____
4. are you a girl? = _____
5. how . . . ? = _____
6. inside = _____
7. to fill = _____
8. correr = _____
9. las lágrimas = _____
10. que = _____
11. qué = _____

Here are the answers:

1. you are sure
2. are you sure?
3. that is a face
4. ¿eres una niña?
5. ¿cómo. . . ?
6. dentro (de)
7. llenar
8. to flow; to run
9. the tears
10. that
11. what

This house does not leave room for errors!
If you missed more than 2, go back and try again.
And if you are not totally confident about **this** and
and **that**, go back and study! Better to learn these
now than later, if you get my drift! When you are
truly ready, you may proceed to Capítulo 16.

« *Las puertas retorcidas. . . las puertas retorcidas* », repite.
« Me recuerdan algo, tú sabes, Francisca. . . ».
« Trata de recordar, Enrique ».
De repente, el hombre viejo y feo abre la
puerta de esta habitación vacía.
« **¡Ah! ¡Los he encontrado, niños!** », se ríe.
¿Cómo podemos salir de esta habitación?
¡El hombre malvado bloquea la salida!
Enrique entra en pánico.
¿Qué tenemos que hacer? ¡No podemos escapar de la habitación!
Lo pienso: la pintura está viva. . .
¿Cómo podemos entrar en ella para escapar
de esta habitación?
« ¡Enrique! ¡Toquemos la pintura viviente! ¡Es nuestra
última esperanza! ¡Rápido! ».
Los dos la tocamos juntos. . .

« The twisted doors . . . the twisted doors, » *he repeats.*
« *They remind me of something, you know, Francisca . . .* »
« *Try to remember, Enrique.* »
Suddenly, the old ugly man opens the
door of this empty room.
« ***Ah! I have found you, children!*** » *he laughs.*
How can we get out of this room?
The wicked man is blocking the exit!
Enrique goes into a panic.
What should we do? We can't escape from the room!
I think it over: the painting is living . . .
How can we get inside it in order to escape
from this room?
« *Enrique! Let's touch the living painting! It is our*
last hope! Quick! »
We both touch it together . . .

algo = something
tú sabes or sabes = you know
tratar de = to try to
tratar de recordar = to try to remember
de repente = suddenly
podemos = we can
malvado = evil; wicked (masculine)
bloquear = to **block** (off)
la salida = the exit
escapar (de) = to **escap**e (from)
para = in order to; for; to
tocar = to touch
rápido = quickly; quick; fast
los dos = both
juntos = together

Now here is how you say **to try to**. You had
better try to learn it now! This is an **-ar** verb.
The endings are **-o**, **-as**, **-a**, **-amos**, **-an**.

trat**ar** de = to try to

yo trat**o** de = I try to; I am trying to; I do try to
tú trat**as** de = you try to; you are trying to; you do try to
usted trat**a** de = you try to; you are trying to; you do try to
él, ella trat**a** de = he, she, it tries to; he is trying to; he does try to
nosotros, nosotras trat**amos** de = we try to; we are trying to; we do try to
ustedes trat**an** de = you try to; you are trying to; you do try to
ellos, ellas trat**an** de = they try to; they are trying to; they do try to

Now take this test. You will surely need this later!

1. you (singular) try to remember = _____ or _____
2. she tries to look at = _____
3. evil = _____
4. the exit = _____
5. I try to run = _____
6. rápido = _____
7. we try to see = _____ or _____
8. you (plural) try to cry = _____
9. he tries to touch = _____
10. something = _____
11. escapar (de) = _____
12. together = _____
13. both = _____

Aquí están las repuestas. (Here are the answers.)

1. tú tratas de recordar or usted trata de recordar
2. ella trata de mirar
3. malvado
4. la salida
5. yo trato de correr
6. quickly
7. nosotros tratamos de ver or nosotras tratamos de ver
8. ustedes tratan de llorar
9. él trata de tocar
10. algo
11. to escape (from)
12. juntos
13. los dos

Do you want to see what happens when Francisca and Enrique
touch the painting? Then make sure you do not miss more
than 2. If you did, go back, study, and take the test again.
Then, when you are ready, you may go on to Capítulo 17
to find out the very strange result that awaits them.

NOTAS

« Dios mío, ¿dónde estamos? », decimos al mismo tiempo.
« Todo está negro. No veo nada ».
« Yo tampoco ».
Poco a poco, nuestros ojos se acostumbran a la oscuridad.
« Espera, Enrique. . . ¿Qué es eso? ¿Qué ves allí? ».
« Eso es una puerta, Francisca ».
Me acerco a la puerta.
« Tienes razón, Enrique. Mírala. . . Es extraña.
¡LA PUERTA ESTÁ RETORCIDA! ».
« ¡Francisca, las puertas retorcidas! Vimos las puertas retorcidas
en la pintura. . . ¡Eso significa que estamos
dentro de la pintura viviente! ».
« ¡Es decir que tocando la pintura,
logramos entrar en ella! ».
Nos miramos el uno al otro. El pobre Enrique comienza a llorar.
« ¿Cómo podemos estar **dentro de** una pintura?
¡Es imposible! », lloriquea el pequeño Enrique.
Sin embargo, sé que ésta es la única explicación.
« ¿Cómo podemos salir de ella? », grita Enrique.
Pero no tengo mucho tiempo para reflexionar porque,
de repente, oímos un terrible chirrido:
¡la puerta retorcida comienza a abrirse por sí misma!

« My goodness, where are we? » we say together.
« Everything is black. I don't see anything. »
« Me neither. »
Little by little, our eyes get used to the darkness.
« Wait, Enrique . . . What is that? What do you see over there? »
« That is a door, Francisca. »
I approach the door.
« You are right, Enrique. Look at it . . . It is strange.
THE DOOR IS TWISTED! *»*
« Francisca, the twisted doors! We saw the twisted doors
in the painting . . . That means that we are
inside the living painting! »
« That is to say that in touching the painting,
we succeeded in entering it! »
We look at one another. Poor Enrique begins to cry.
*« How can we be **inside** a painting?*
It is impossible! » whimpers little Enrique.
Yet I know that this is the only explanation.
« How can we get out of it? » Enrique cries.
But I do not have much time to think (it) over, because
suddenly, we hear a terrible creaking (noise):
the twisted door begins to open by itself!

al mismo tiempo = at the same time; together
todo = all; everything
no veo or yo **no** veo = I do **not** see
no veo **nada** or yo **no** veo **nada** = I do **not** see **anything**
¿qué es **eso**? = what is **that**?
* ¿qué es **esto**? = what is **this**?
allí = over there
tienes razón = you are right
eso significa = **that** means
* **esto** significa = **this** means
es decir = that is to say
otro = another (masculine)
pobre = **po**or
sin embargo = however; nevertheless; yet
mucho = **much**; a lot of
el **tiem**po = (the) **tim**e
mucho tiempo = a lot of time
reflexionar = to think; to think over; to **refle**ct (on)
porque = because
por sí misma = by itself (feminine)

If you know what is good for you, you had
better learn how to say **to be right**. Watch out!
In Spanish you say **I have reason**, not I **am** right.

tener razón = to be right

yo **tengo** razón = I am right
tú **tienes** razón = you are right
usted **tiene** razón = you are right
él, ella **tiene** razón = he, she is right
nosotros, nosotras **tenemos** razón = we are right
ustedes **tienen** razón = you are right
ellos, ellas **tienen** razón = they are right

Now here is another verb that you have seen many
times: **ver**. Study it well. You will see why later!

ver = to see

yo ve**o** = I see; I am seeing; I do see
tú **ves** = you see; you are seeing; you do see
usted v**e** = you see; you are seeing; you do see
él, ella v**e** = he, she, it sees; he is seeing; he does see
nosotros, nosotras v**emos** = we see; we are seeing; we do see
ustedes **ven** = you see; you are seeing; you do see
ellos, ellas v**en** = they see; they are seeing; they do see

Take this test.

1. otro = _____
2. él tiene razón = _____
3. he sees = _____
4. ¿qué es esto? = _____
5. he is right = _____
6. I am right = _____
7. mucho = _____
8. el tiempo = _____
9. we are right = _____ or _____
10. eso significa = _____
11. we see = _____ or _____
12. todo = _____

54

Aquí están las respuestas. (Here are the answers.)

1. another
2. he is right
3. él ve
4. what is this?
5. él tiene razón
6. yo tengo razón
7. much; a lot of
8. (the) time
9. nosotros tenemos razón or nosotras tenemos razón
10. that means
11. nosotros vemos or nosotras vemos
12. all; everything

If you missed more than 2, go back and study
hard! Then take the test again. When you are ready,
you may go on to Capítulo 18 to find out about
the opening, creaking, twisted door!

Enrique se arroja sobre mí. Percibo el temblor
de su pobre cuerpo.
Trato de ser valiente, pero francamente,
estoy asustada.
La puerta retorcida continúa su chirrido atroz. . .
Tengo ganas de taparme los oídos.
A pesar del terror, caminamos hacia la puerta.
De repente, oigo un grito de Enrique:
« ¡Francisca, mira! ¡Es el exterior! ».
Estando la puerta retorcida completamente abierta,
podemos ver el cielo.
Avanzamos otra vez dos o tres pasos.
Estamos afuera.
« Mira el cielo, Francisca. . . Está todo morado.
Y las nubes son enormes y amarillas.
Y el viento sopla fuerte en mis oídos.
Y la. . . ».
« ¡Detente, Enrique! ¡Escucha bien! », susurro yo.
« ¡Se podría decir que el viento está silbando *tu nombre*! ».
En efecto, escuchamos: « E n r i q u e. . . E n r i q u e. . . E n r i q u e. . . ».

*Enrique throws himself upon me. I perceive the trembling
of his poor (little) body.
I try to be courageous, but frankly,
I am frightened.
The twisted door continues its atrocious creaking . . .
I feel like covering my ears.
Despite this terror, we walk toward the door.
Suddenly, I hear a cry from Enrique:
« Francisca, look! It is the outside! »
The twisted door being completely open,
we can see the sky.*

We advance again two or three steps.
We are outside.
« Look at the sky, Francisca . . . It is all purple.
And the clouds are enormous and yellow.
And the wind is blowing hard in my ears.
And the . . . »
« Stop, Enrique! Listen carefully! » I whisper.
« One would say that the wind is whistling your name! »
Indeed we hear, « E n r i q u e . . . E n r i q u e . . . E n r i q u e . . . »

arrojar**se** = to throw **oneself**
* arrojar = to throw; to hurl
el cuerpo = the body
valiente = courageous
tengo ganas de = I feel like
* tener ganas de = to feel like
* él tiene ganas de llorar = he feels like crying
a pesar de = despite
caminar = to walk
el **exterior** = the **exterior**; the outside
el cielo = the sky
otra vez = again (think: another time)
un paso = a step; a pace
una nube = a cloud
el **vient**o = the wind (think: **vent**ilation)
soplar = to blow
silbar = to whistle
morad**o** = purple (**masculine**)
amarill**o** = yellow (**masculine**)
* roj**o** = red (**masculine**)
* verde = green (masculine or feminine)
* azul = blue (masculine or feminine)
* marrón = brown (masculine or feminine)
* blanc**a** = white (**feminine**) (think: blank)
* negr**o** = black (**masculine**)
* rosado or rosa = pink (think: **ros**e)
* anaranjado or naranja = orange
* gris = gray (masculine or feminine)

If I tell you that **yo tengo ganas de llorar** means *I feel like crying*,
and **él tiene ganas de llorar** means *he feels like crying*, then see
if you can figure out how to do the sentences below yourself!
Hint: You have to conjugate the **tener** (**to have**) verb first.

1. I feel like crying
2. you (singular) feel like crying
3. he, she feels like crying
4. we feel like crying
5. you (plural) feel like crying
6. they feel like crying

So, all you do is conjugate the **tener** verb and then add **ganas de** followed by the verb's infinitive form which in this example is *to cry* or **llorar**. That's it! Study the answers below.

1. yo ***tengo* ganas de** llorar
2. tú ***tienes* ganas de** llorar or usted ***tiene* ganas de** llorar
3. él, ella ***tiene* ganas de** llorar
4. nosotros, nosotras ***tenemos* ganas de** llorar
5. ustedes ***tienen* ganas de** llorar
6. ellos, ellas ***tienen* ganas de** llorar

Now take this test.

1. nosotros tenemos ganas de silbar = _____
2. las nubes son moradas = _____
3. the sky is blue = _____
4. la puerta es amarilla = _____
5. they feel like looking = _____
6. las nubes son rosadas = _____
7. I feel like crying = _____
8. you (singular, familiar) feel like walking = _____
9. naranja = _____
10. marrón = _____
11. blanco = _____
12. green = _____
13. black (feminine) = _____
14. red (feminine) = _____
15. to blow = _____
16. caminar = _____
17. gray = _____

Aquí están las respuestas:

1. we feel like whistling
2. the clouds are purple
3. el cielo es azul
4. the door is yellow
5. ellos tienen ganas de mirar or ellas tienen ganas de mirar

6. the clouds are pink
7. yo tengo ganas de llorar
8. tú tienes ganas de caminar
9. orange
10. brown
11. white
12. verde
13. negra
14. roja
15. soplar
16. to walk
17. gris

Hard enough for you?
You cannot go on if you missed more than three.
If you did, go back and study. Then take the test
again. When you are ready, you may proceed at
your own risk to Capítulo 19 to find out what
Francisca and Enrique are going to find!

« Dios mío, Enrique. Mira a nuestro alrededor.
¡Estamos en un cementerio! ».
El viento continúa silbando: « Enrique. . . Enrique. . . ».
Hay tumbas por todos lados. Hay lápidas
de todos los tamaños, de todo tipo.
« ¿Qué significa este cementerio? », dice Enrique
con un aire preocupado.
« No me gusta. Quiero regresar », dice como un niño consentido.
« ¿Quieres regresar? No me hagas reír, Enrique.
¿Adónde quieres regresar exactamente? ».
« Yo no sé, pero. . . ».
« Oh, cállate. Tú sabes muy bien que. . . ».
Interrumpo mi respuesta, porque de inmediato, mi vista
es atraída por una lápida que no es como las otras.
En efecto, su epitafio es bastante curioso, como
se puede ver por la siguiente inscripción:

**Él no esperó
que la puerta retorcida
se abriera sola
¡Peor para él! Se quedará
aquí para siempre**

Nos miramos. ¿Qué significa eso?
¿**Quién** no esperó?

60

« My goodness, Enrique. Look around us.
We are in a cemetery! »
The wind continues whistling, « Enrique . . . Enrique . . . »
There are tombs everywhere. There are tombstones
of all sizes, of all sorts.
« What's this cemetery? » says Enrique
with a worried look.
« I don't like (it). I want to go back, » he says like a spoiled child.
« You want to go back? Don't make me laugh, Enrique.
Where do you want to go back to, exactly? »
« I don't know but . . . »
« Oh, be quiet. You know very well that . . . »
I cut short my reply because my eyes are immediately
attracted to a tombstone that is not like the others.
Indeed, its epitaph is quite curious as
can be witnessed by the following inscription:

He did not wait
for the twisted door
to open by itself
Too bad for him! He will stay
here forever

We look at each other. What does that mean?
Who *did not wait?*

alrededor = around
el viento = the wind
hay = there is; there are
por todos lados = everywhere
todos = all (masculine plural)
lados = sides
preocupado = worried (masculine)
no me gusta = I don't like (it)
quiero = I want
regresar = to go back
consentido = spoiled (masculine)
no me hagas = don't make me
* hacer = to do; to make
¿adónde. . . ? = where . .˙. ?
de **inmediat**o = **immediat**ely
mi vista = my sight; my eyes
atraer = to attract
siguiente = following
esperar = to wait (for)
¿quién? = who?

Now you are going to learn the **to do** or **to make** verb, **hacer**.
Watch out, because it is tricky. But if you want to find
out what happens in the cemetery, learn it now!

hac**er** = to do; to make

yo hag**o** = I do; I make
tú hac**es** = you do; you make
usted hac**e** = you do; you make
él, ella hac**e** = he, she, it does; he, she, it makes
nosotros, nosotras hac**emos** = we do; we make
ustedes hac**en** = you do; you make
ellos, ellas hac**en** = they do; they make

Did you see how tricky **yo hago** is? But
to get anywhere in this place, you had
better remember this conjugation!
Now take this test.

1. immediately = _____
2. por todos lados = _____
3. esperar = _____
4. my sight; my eyes = _____
5. he makes = _____
6. I do = _____
7. you (plural) make = _____
8. they do = _____
9. you (singular) make = _____ or _____
10. preocupada = _____
11. we do = _____ or _____
12. atraer = _____

Aquí están las respuestas:

1. de inmediato
2. everywhere
3. to wait (for)
4. mi vista
5. él hace
6. yo hago
7. ustedes hacen
8. ellos hacen or ellas hacen
9. tú haces or usted hace
10. worried
11. nosotros hacemos or nosotras hacemos
12. to attract

If you missed more than one, go back and take the test again. Then, when you are really ready, you may go on and try to decipher the epitaph in Capítulo 20!

« **Él no esperó que la puerta retorcida se abriera sola** », susurra Enrique.
Veo la cara de Enrique ponerse completamente pálida. Su labio inferior
tiembla. Él mira hacia el cielo como si fuera a obtener una
respuesta lógica a todas sus preguntas. Baja sus ojos azules
y luego me mira fijamente.
« Soy yo, Francisca. ¡Soy yo el que no esperó que
la puerta retorcida se abriera sola! ¡Francisca, creo que he estado
en esta casa vieja por mucho más de dos semanas! ».
Lo tomo suavemente por los hombros.
« ¿Enrique, recuerdas algo?
¡Cuéntame! ».
Enrique me mira nuevamente y me contesta,
con mucha calma:
« Sí, recuerdo algo. . . ».

« *He did not wait for the twisted door to open by itself*, » *whispers Enrique.*
I see Enrique's face become completely pale. His lower lip
trembles. He looks toward the sky as if he were to obtain a
logical answer to all his questions. He lowers his blue eyes
and then he fixes his gaze upon me.
« It is me, Francisca. It is me who did not wait for
the twisted door to open by itself! Francisca, I think that I have been
in this old house for much more than two weeks! »
I take him gently by the shoulders.
« Enrique, do you remember something?
Tell me! »
Enrique looks at me again and he answers me
very calmly:
« Yes, I remember something . . . »

susurrar = to whisper
la cara = the face
el labio = the lip
como si = as if
una respuesta = an answer; a reply
una pregunta = a question
bajar = to lower
los ojos = the eyes
luego = then; later (on)
mucho más = much more
más = more
lo = him; it
tomo = I take
los hombros = the shoulders
contestar = to answer; to reply
con calma = calmly

Now you must learn the other parts of the body if
you want to find out what poor Enrique remembers!

la cabeza = the head
la nariz = the nose
la boca = the mouth
la mejilla = the cheek
el pelo = the hair
el brazo = the arm
la **man**o = the hand (think: **man**ufacture)
la pierna = the leg
el pie = the foot
las orejas = the ears

Study hard to learn all these words.
You won't be sorry later! Now take this test.

1. los ojos = _____
2. the nose = _____
3. the ears = _____
4. la cabeza = _____
5. the lip = _____
6. the foot = _____
7. the hand = _____
8. el pelo = _____
9. the arm = _____
10. el pie = _____
11. the mouth = _____
12. la pierna = _____

Aquí están las respuestas:

1. the eyes
2. la nariz
3. las orejas
4. the head
5. el labio
6. el pie
7. la mano
8. the hair
9. el brazo
10. the foot
11. la boca
12. the leg

If you missed more than 2, go back and study.
Then take the test again. When you are ready,
you may go on to Capítulo 21.

El cielo se pone completamente negro a nuestro alrededor.
Enormes nubes verdes cruzan el cielo
a una velocidad espeluznante. Pero, es especialmente el viento el que
nos hace perder el ánimo, porque silba muy claramente y con una
fuerza espantosa: « **¡ENRIQUE. . . ENRIQUE!** ».
« ¡Rápido, Enrique! ¡Esta tormenta siniestra va a matarnos!
¡Tú **debes** recordar algo! ».
Sin emoción, sin decir una palabra, el pequeño Enrique avanza
lentamente hacia la lápida. Extiende su pequeña mano
y comienza a remover el polvo que cubre la
parte inferior de la piedra.
« ¡Enrique, éste no es realmente el momento para hacer la limpieza! »,
digo casi llorando.
« ¿Me escuchas? ¡Enrique! ¡Respóndeme! ».
Enrique se vuelve hacia mí por un instante.
Entonces, (él) da dos pasos hacia atrás.
¡De repente, la veo! ¡Hay otra inscripción!

The sky becomes completely black around us.
Huge green clouds cross the sky
at a horrifying speed. But it is especially the wind that
causes us to lose heart because it whistles very clearly and with an
*appalling force, « **ENRIQUE . . . ENRIQUE!** »*
« Quick, Enrique! This sinister storm is going to kill us!
*You **must** remember something! »*
Without emotion, without saying a word, little Enrique advances
slowly toward the tombstone. He holds out his little hand
and starts to remove the dust that covers the
bottom portion of the stone.
« Enrique, this is really not the time to do the cleaning! »
I say almost crying.
« Do you hear me? Enrique! Answer me! »
Enrique turns toward me for an instant.
Then, he takes two steps backwards.
Suddenly, I see it! There is another inscription!

alrededor = around
las nubes = the clouds
cruzar = to cross
una **veloci**dad = a speed; a **veloci**ty
perder = to lose
ánimo = spirit; courage; heart
espantoso = appalling; dreadful; frightening (masculine)
matar = to kill
sin = without
el polvo = the dust
cubrir = to cover
la piedra = the stone
la limpieza = the cleaning
casi = almost
volverse = to turn
entonces = then
hacia **atrás** = backwards
* atrás = backwards; behind

Now you are going to learn the expression **hay** which
comes from the verb **haber**. (See Capítulo 31.)
Hay means **there is** or **there are**.
Here are some examples:

hay una tumba = there is a tomb
hay un cielo rojo = there is a red sky
hay unas nubes = there are some clouds
hay dos manos = there are two hands

Get it? Now take this test!

1. there is a door = _____
2. hay una inscripción = _____
3. cruzar = _____
4. la velocidad = _____
5. alrededor = _____
6. casi = _____
7. hacia atrás = _____
8. without = _____
9. to kill = _____
10. then = _____
11. the stone = _____
12. el polvo = _____

Aquí están las respuestas:

1. hay una puerta
2. there is an inscription
3. to cross
4. the speed
5. around
6. almost
7. backwards
8. sin
9. matar
10. entonces
11. la piedra
12. the dust

If you missed more than 1, go back, study, and take the test again. Otherwise, you cannot go on to Capítulo 22 to find out what this new inscription reveals!

Nosotros no le prestamos atención ni a la terrible tormenta que se aproxima,
ni al viento infernal que continúa silbando el nombre de Enrique.
Nuestra atención está concentrada sobre esta espantosa lápida gris que ha
escondido su secreto bajo el polvo por
un tiempo indeterminado:

El espíritu de
Enrique descansa aquí
Para liberarlo
presiona *Aquí*

« ¡Ah, lo sabía, Francisca! ¡Aquí está la prueba de que he estado
en esta casa por mucho más de dos semanas!
¡Mi nombre está inscrito en esta lápida! ».
Enrique tiembla de terror.
¿Cómo puedo consolarlo?
Después de todo, su nombre está en efecto grabado en esta piedra. . .
¿Qué significa esto? ¿Será que mi pobre Enrique
ya no es de este mundo? Me esfuerzo en esconderle mis
verdaderos sentimientos a Enrique. Sería espantoso estar en su lugar.
Me armo de valor y le digo:
« No te preocupes, Enrique. Vamos a salir de esta situación.
¡Vas a ver! ».
El pequeño Enrique trata de sonreír. . . pero no lo logra.
Veo pequeñas gotas de sudor formándose en su frente.
« Francisca, ¿es demasiado tarde? ¿Estoy
muerto ya? ¡Ayúdame! ¡Te lo suplico! ».
Yo no puedo más.
Las palabras de Enrique me conmueven.
Muy a mi pesar, empiezo a llorar.
Enrique se da cuenta de lo que me ha hecho.

Un poco avergonzado, se yergue y camina como
un pequeño soldado hacia la tumba.
Lo escucho releyendo la inscripción en voz alta:

**El espíritu de
Enrique descansa aquí
Para liberarlo
presiona *Aquí***

« ¿Dónde hay que presionar? », dice perplejo.
« ¿No ves, Enrique? », le respondo lloriqueando.
« ¡Es obvio! ».

*We pay neither attention to the dreadful storm that approaches,
nor to the infernal wind that continues whistling Enrique's name.
Our attention is centered upon this dreadful gray tombstone that has
hidden its secret under the dust for
an undetermined (amount of) time:*

**The spirit of
Enrique rests here
In order to free it
press *Here***

*« Ah, I knew it, Francisca! Here is the proof that I have been
in this house for much more than two weeks!
My name is inscribed on this tombstone! »
Enrique shivers with terror.
How can I comfort him?
After all, his name is indeed engraved on this stone . . .
What does this mean? Could it be that my poor Enrique
is no longer of this world? I force myself to hide my
true feelings from Enrique. It would be dreadful to be in his place.
I summon up courage and I say to him:
« Don't worry, Enrique. We are going to get out of this situation.
You're going to see! »
Little Enrique tries to smile . . . but he doesn't succeed.
I see little drops of sweat forming on his forehead.
« Francisca, is it too late? Am I
already dead? Help me! I beg you! »
I can't go on any more.
Enrique's words overcome me with emotion.
Much to my regret, I begin to cry.
Enrique realizes what he has done to me.*

A little embarrassed, he straightens himself up and walks like
a little soldier toward the tomb.
I hear him re-reading the inscription aloud:

The spirit of
Enrique rests here
In order to free it
press *Here*

« Where do we have to press? » he says perplexed.
« Don't you see, Enrique? » I answer him (while) sniveling.
« It's obvious! »

no. . . ni. . . ni = neither . . . nor
prestar atención = to pay attention
terrible = dreadful; terrible
la tormenta = the (thunder)storm
el **nom**bre = the **nam**e
sobre = on; upon
esconder = to hide
bajo = under
el e**spírit**u = the **spirit**
descansar = to rest
aquí = here
la **pr**ueba = the **pr**oof
después de todo = after all
* después = after; afterwards
ya no = no longer; not any more
este mundo = this world
una gota = a drop
el sudor = the sweat
la frente = the forehead
a mi pesar = to my regret
pesar = regret; sorrow
llorar = to cry
poco = little
avergonzar = to embarrass
se y**ergu**e = he rises up; he straightens himself up
* **ergu**irse = to rise up; to straighten up (oneself)

Now you are going to learn two more **-er** verbs.
Their endings are **-o**, **-es**, **-e**, **-emos**, **-en**.

escond**er** = to hide

yo escond**o** = I hide; I am hiding; I do hide
tú escond**es** = you hide; you are hiding; you do hide
usted escond**e** = you hide; you are hiding; you do hide
él, ella escond**e** = he, she, it hides; he is hiding; he does hide
nosotros, nosotras escond**emos** = we hide; we are hiding; we do hide
ustedes escond**en** = you hide; you are hiding; you do hide
ellos, ellas escond**en** = they hide; they are hiding; they do hide

respond**er** = to answer

yo respond**o** = I answer; I am answering; I do answer
tú respond**es** = you answer; you are answering; you do answer
usted respond**e** = you answer; you are answering; you do answer
él, ella respond**e** = he, she, it answers; he is answering; he does answer
nosotros, nosotras respond**emos** = we answer; we are answering; we do answer
ustedes respond**en** = you answer; you are answering; you do answer
ellos, ellas respond**en** = they answer; they are answering; they do answer

Now is the time to learn these
verbs. You will see why later!

Study hard and take this test.

1. pesar = _____
2. el mundo = _____
3. the proof = _____
4. the sweat = _____
5. avergonzar = _____
6. to cry = _____
7. una gota = _____
8. under = _____
9. terrible; dreadful = _____
10. I hide = _____
11. ellos responden = _____
12. you (singular, familiar) hide = _____
13. he answers = _____
14. nosotros respondemos = _____
15. we hide = _____ or _____
16. you (plural) answer = _____

Aquí están las respuestas:

1. regret; sorrow
2. the world
3. la prueba
4. el sudor
5. to embarrass
6. llorar
7. a drop
8. bajo
9. terrible
10. yo escondo
11. they answer
12. tú escondes
13. él responde
14. we answer
15. nosotros escondemos or nosotras escondemos
16. ustedes responden

If you missed more than two, you cannot go on
to Capítulo 23 to find out where (and what) they
need to press in order to free Enrique's spirit!
You must study and take the test again.
Then when you have passed the test,
you may proceed to Capítulo 23!

NOTAS

« ¡**Aquí**, Enrique! », le digo olvidando mi tristeza.
« Mira cómo la inscripción de la palabra **Aquí** está inclinada de una
manera curiosa. ¡Además, la inscripción dice claramente presionar **Aquí**! ».
Orgullosa de mi misma, me apuro a presionar
sobre esta palabra curiosamente formada. . .
¡Pero este movimiento es interrumpido bruscamente
por una ráfaga de viento que me hace girar como un trompo!
Todavía un poco mareada, me doy cuenta de que soy
la única víctima del viento. A Enrique no lo toca.
Él ni siquiera es consciente de lo que me sucedió.
« ¡Oh, qué viento tan extraño!
Si no supiera. . . ».
« ¡Espera, Francisca! », grita Enrique.
Parece que él ve algo.
Enrique se inclina para poder
examinar de cerca la inscripción, **Aquí**.
Luego me mira con un aire perplejo.
« Tienes razón, Francisca. Esta palabra está grabada de una manera peculiar.
¡Las letras **A** e **I** parecen formar los lados de un objeto! ».
Instintivamente, él coloca la punta de los dedos sobre las letras.
Yo lo veo palpar estas letras con cuidado.
De pronto, se levanta gritando:
« ¡Francisca, esto es una puerta retorcida en miniatura,
camuflada para que parezcan letras! ».
« **¡Enrique, entonces aquí es dónde tenemos que presionar
para salvarte!** ».
Yo salto hacia la lápida para
presionar rápidamente esta asombrosa fabricación.
¡Pum!
Veo una luz deslumbrante acompañada de un
dolor abdominal que me corta el aliento.
¡Es el pequeño Enrique quien me está atacando!
« **¡NO! ¡DETENTE, FRANCISCA!** ¿Recuerdas
el epitafio? ¡Tienes que esperar que la puerta retorcida se abra
por sí misma! ¡Si no, serás una prisionera como yo
en esta casa diabólica para siempre! ».
Finalmente. . .
Enrique recuerda por qué está prisionero:
él abrió una puerta retorcida. Eso es todo. Un acto realmente inocente.
Y ahora, él me acaba de salvar de
un destino igual al suyo.

*« **Aquí** (Here), Enrique! » I say to him forgetting my sadness.*
*« Look how the inscription of the word **Aquí** is slanted in a*
*curious way. What's more, the epitaph clearly says to press **Aquí**! »*
Proud of myself, I hurry to press down
on this curiously fashioned word . . .
But this motion is abruptly interrupted
by a gust of wind that causes me to spin around like a top!
Still a little bit dizzy, I realize that I am
the only victim of the wind. It doesn't touch Enrique.
He isn't even aware of what happened to me.
« Oh, how the wind is bizarre!
If I didn't know . . . »
« Wait, Francisca! » cries out Enrique.
He seems to see something.
Enrique leans over in order to be able
*to closely examine the inscription, **Aquí**.*
Then he looks at me with a perplexed air.
« You are right, Francisca. This word is engraved in a peculiar way.
*The letters **A** and **I** seem to form the sides of an object! »*
Instinctively, he places the tip of his fingers on the letters.
I see him palpate these letters with care.
Suddenly, he gets up (while) shouting,
« Francisca, this is a miniature twisted door
disguised to look like letters! »
*« **Enrique, then here's where we have to press***
in order to save you! »
I jump toward the tombstone in order to
quickly press down on this astonishing fabrication.
Bang!
I see a dazzling light accompanied by an
abdominal pain that knocks the breath out of me.
It is little Enrique who is attacking me!
*« **NO! STOP, FRANCISCA!** Remember*
the epitaph? You have to wait for the twisted door to open
***by itself!** If not, you will be a prisoner like me*
in this diabolical house forever! »
***Finally** . . .*
Enrique remembers why he is (a) prisoner:
he opened a twisted door. That's all. A really innocent act.
And now, he just saved me from
the same destiny as his.

aquí = here
olvidar = to forget
la tristeza = the sadness
inclinada = tilted; sloped; slanted (feminine)
la **maner**a = the way; the **man**n**er**
me apuro = to hurry up (myself)
presionar = to **pres**s (down) (on)
una ráfaga de viento = a gust of wind
tocar = to touch
ni siquiera = not even
suceder = to happen
inclinarse = to lean over
poder = to be able to
de cerca = closely
cerca = close; near(by)
formar = to **form**
el lado = the side
colocar = to place; to put
salvar = to **sav**e
una luz = a light
el dolor = the pain
cortarme el aliento = to knock the breath out of me
* cortar = to cut
el aliento = the breath
tener que = to have to; must
por qué = why
el **destin**o = the **destin**y; the fate
igual = same; equal (masculine or feminine)

How do you feel about **-ar** verbs?
See how well you do now with the verbs below.
If you remember your endings, you
should have no trouble conjugating the
following verbs:

salvar
formar
cortar

After you conjugate these three verbs,
take this test!

1. el lado = _____
2. la tristeza = _____
3. close = _____
4. the pain = _____
5. to form = _____
6. the gust of wind = _____
7. the light = _____
8. the breath = _____
9. to save = _____
10. to have to = _____
11. here = _____

Aquí están las respuestas:

salv**ar** = to save
yo salv**o** = I save; I am saving; I do save
tú salv**as** = you save; you are saving; you do save
usted salv**a** = you save; you are saving; you do save
él, ella salv**a** = he, she, it saves; he is saving; he does save
nosotros, nosotras salv**amos** = we save; we are saving; we do save
ustedes salv**an** = you save; you are saving; you do save
ellos, ellas salv**an** = they save; they are saving; they do save

form**ar** = to form
yo form**o** = I form; I am forming; I do form
tú form**as** = you form; you are forming; you do form
usted form**a** = you form; you are forming; you do form
él, ella form**a** = he, she, it forms; he is forming; he does form
nosotros, nosotras form**amos** = we form; we are forming; we do form
ustedes form**an** = you form; you are forming; you do form
ellos, ellas form**an** = they form; they are forming; they do form

cort**ar** = to cut
yo cort**o** = I cut; I am cutting; I do cut
tú cort**as** = you cut; you are cutting; you do cut
usted cort**a** = you cut; you are cutting; you do cut
él, ella cort**a** = he, she, it cuts; he is cutting; he does cut
nosotros, nosotras cort**amos** = we cut; we are cutting; we do cut
ustedes cort**an** = you cut; you are cutting; you do cut
ellos, ellas cort**an** = they cut; they are cutting; they do cut

1. the side
2. the sadness
3. cerca
4. el dolor
5. formar
6. la ráfaga de viento
7. la luz
8. el aliento
9. salvar
10. tener que
11. aquí

You are allowed to miss only one on the vocabulary words and none on the conjugation in order to go on to Capítulo 24. So, study and take the test again if you want to find out what happens in this eerie cemetery!

Recupero el aliento. Me pongo de pie.
La tormenta está cada vez más cerca. Un relámpago pinta su
fina trayectoria sobre el cielo muy oscuro. Lo siguen los truenos con
un estruendo que lastima mis oídos. El viento silba:
« Enrique. . . Enrique », haciendo remolinos de polvo y escombros.
Sé intuitivamente que no tenemos mucho tiempo.
Tenemos que salir de este cementerio o moriremos.
Esta pequeña puerta retorcida es nuestra única esperanza.
Nosotros mismos no podemos abrirla. ¿Cómo hacemos para que se abra?
Voy hacia la minúscula puerta.
Trato de examinarla de cerca.
¿Se nos ha pasado por alto una pista?
Enrique viene a mi lado. Él no sabe que estamos
en peligro mortal. Es mejor que no se dé cuenta de esto.
Lo veo reexaminar la pequeña puerta.
« Francisca, creo que he encontrado algo escrito
en esta puerta. Es muy pequeño. . . Apenas puedo leerlo ».
Él deletrea (cada letra) lentamente y con cuidado:
« s-e-r ».
¡Qué irónico! ¿Hay alguien ahí que está burlándose de nosotros?

◈

I catch my breath. I stand up.
The storm is closer and closer. A flash of lightning paints its
thin trajectory against the very dark sky. The thunder follows with
a crash that hurts my ears. The wind whistles,
« Enrique . . . Enrique, » (while) making whirlwinds of dust and debris.
I know intuitively that we don't have much time.
We have to get out of this cemetery or we will die.
This little twisted door is our only hope.
We cannot open it ourselves. How do we make it open?
I go toward the tiny door.
I try to examine it close up.
Have we missed a clue?
Enrique comes by my side. He doesn't know that we are
in mortal danger. It's better that he doesn't realize this.
I see him re-examine the little door.
« Francisca, I believe that I have found something written
on this door. It is very small . . . I can barely read it. »
He spells out each letter slowly and carefully:
« t-o b-e »
How ironic! Is there someone out there (who is) mocking us?

◈

ponerse de pie = to stand up
* pie = foot
una tormenta = a (thunder)storm
un relámpago = a flash of lightning
pintar = to paint
fina = thin (feminine)
seguir = to follow
los truenos = (the) thunder
* un trueno = a thunderclap; a clap of thunder
un estruendo = a crash (of thunder)
haciendo = doing; making (gerund)
tenemos que = we have to
* tener que = to have to
salir = to get out; to leave
morir = to die (think: **mor**tal)
de **cerca** = **close**ly; **close** up
pasar por alto = to miss; to pass over
una pista = a clue
el lado = the side
darse cuenta de = to realize
encontrar = to find
apenas = barely; hardly
de**letr**ear = to spell (out) (think: **lett**er)
cada = each
la **letr**a = the **lett**er (of the alphabet)
lenta**mente** = slow**ly**
con cuidado = carefully; with care
alguien = someone; somebody
ahí = there

If you know what is good for you,
you must learn to conjugate the verb **salir**.
It is an **-ir** verb. Do you remember the
endings for **-ir** verbs? But watch out! One of the
conjugations of **salir** is not typical of **-ir** verbs.

sal**ir** = to go out; to leave; to get out; to exit; to come out

yo salg**o** = I exit; I am exiting; I do exit
tú sal**es** = you exit; you are exiting; you do exit
usted sal**e** = you exit; you are exiting; you do exit
él, ella, sal**e** = he, she, it exits; he is exiting; he does exit
nosotros, nosotras sal**imos** = we exit; we are exiting; we do exit
ustedes sal**en** = you exit; you are exiting; you do exit
ellos, ellas sal**en** = they exit; they are exiting; they do exit

Now take this test.

1. tenemos que = _____
2. a thunderstorm = _____
3. the clue = _____
4. un estruendo = _____
5. to get out = _____
6. you (singular) have to leave = _____ or _____
7. they have to find = _____ or _____
8. nosotros tenemos que salir = _____
9. to spell (out) = _____
10. carefully = _____
11. each = _____
12. alguien = _____

Aquí están las respuestas:

1. we have to
2. una tormenta
3. la pista
4. a crash (of thunder)
5. salir
6. tú tienes que salir or usted tiene que salir
7. ellos tienen que encontrar or ellas tienen que encontrar
8. we have to get out
9. deletrear
10. con cuidado
11. cada
12. someone; somebody

You are only allowed to miss
one in order to go on to Capítulo 25.
So, study and take the test again if you
want to discover who might be mocking
Francisca and Enrique in the cemetery!

Ser. . . Una referencia shakespeariana que se burla de nosotros.
Afortunadamente, Enrique es demasiado pequeño para comprender. . .
Los incesantes vientos huracanados me recuerdan mi mortalidad.
Debo actuar rápidamente. Voy a darle a la pequeña puerta retorcida
lo que ella quiere para poder salvarnos.
Me arrodillo frente a la puerta en miniatura y declaro:

« ser = to be
yo soy = I. . . »

De repente, hay una ráfaga de viento tan intensa que es
intolerable. Me cubro la cara con las manos
para protegerme y entonces oigo la monstruosa voz del viento:

« ¡ENRIQUE. . . ENRIQUE. . . ENRIQUE! ».

¡Pienso por un instante y **finalmente** comprendo!
« ¡Ahora lo entiendo!
¡Enrique, el viento está silbando tu nombre para decirte que
tienes que ser tú el que haga que la puerta retorcida se abra!
¡No yo!
¡Tu **existencia**, tu bien**estar** están en juego! ».
Parece que Enrique comprende. A su vez,
se arrodilla frente a la puerta retorcida. . .
De repente, comienza a hacer mucho frío.
Sentimos una vibración alrededor de nosotros.
« Francisca, **¿qué es eso?** ».
Entonces, oímos una voz demoníaca que resuena
como un trueno:

**« ¡Ah, pequeño Enrique! ¡Francisca está equivocada!
¡Si la escuchas, los dos morirán! ».**

◈

To be . . . *A Shakespearean reference that mocks us.*
Fortunately, Enrique is too little to understand . . .
The incessant gale force winds bring to mind my mortality.
I must act quickly. I am going to give the little twisted door
what it wants in order (to be able) to save us.
I kneel down in front of the miniature door and I declare:

« to be = ser
I am = yo . . . »

Suddenly, there is a gust of wind so intense that it is
intolerable. I cover my face with my hands
in order to protect myself and then I hear the monstrous voice of the wind,

« *ENRIQUE . . . ENRIQUE . . . ENRIQUE!* »

*I think for an instant and **finally** I understand!*
« Now I get it!
Enrique, the wind is whistling your name in order to tell you that
it has to be you that makes the twisted door open!
Not me!
*Your **existence**, your well-**being** are at stake! »*
It seems that Enrique understands. In turn,
he kneels down in front of the twisted door . . .
Suddenly, it starts to get very cold.
We feel a vibration around us.
*« Francisca, **what is that?** »*
Then, we hear a demonic voice that resonates
like a clap of thunder:

« *Ah, little Enrique! Francisca is wrong!*
***If you listen to her, you will both die!* »**

◈

burlarse de = to make fun of; to mock (think: **burl**esque)
a**fortuna**damente = **fortuna**tely; luckily
* la **fortun**a = the **fortun**e; the luck
comprender = to understand (think: **compre**he**nd**)
los vientos huracanados = the gale force winds
recordar = to remember; to remind; to bring to mind
deber = must
actuar = to **act**
poder = to be able; can
ar**rodilla**rse = to **knee**l (down)
* la rodilla = the knee
frente a = in front of; opposite
cubrir = to cover
proteger = to **prote**ct
la **vo**z = the **vo**ice
lo entiendo = I understand; I get it
estar en **juego** = to be at stake
* juego = game
parecer = to look; to look like; to seem
hace frío = it's cold (weather)
* hace calor = it's hot (weather)
* hace viento = it's windy
estar equivocad**a** = to be wrong (**feminine**)
* estar equivocad**o** = to be wrong (**masculine**)
* tener razón = to be right
* no tener razón = to be wrong

In Capítulo 17, you learned that the expression
to be right is **tener razón**. **To be wrong** can either be
no tener razón or **estar equivocado**. Get it?

Examples:
yo **estoy equivocada** = I am wrong
yo **no tengo razón** = I am wrong

Study hard and then take this test.

1. él parece pequeño = _____
2. hace viento = _____
3. ella parece un niño = _____
4. the knee = _____
5. the voice = _____
6. in front of = _____
7. comprender = _____
8. it's cold (weather) = _____

9. it's hot (weather) = _____

10. it seems big = _____

11. cubrir = _____

12. actuar = _____

13. they look very small = _____

14. you (plural) are wrong = _____ or _____

15. we are right = _____ or _____

16. I am wrong (feminine) = _____ or _____

Aquí están las respuestas:

1. he looks little; he seems little
2. it's windy
3. she looks like a (little) boy
4. la rodilla
5. la voz
6. frente a
7. to understand
8. hace frío
9. hace calor
10. parece grande
11. to cover
12. to act
13. parecen muy pequeños or parecen muy pequeñas
14. ustedes están equivocados or ustedes no tienen razón
15. nosotros tenemos razón or nosotras tenemos razón
16. yo estoy equivocada or yo no tengo razón

If you missed more than two on this test, you must
study and take the test again. Then, when you are
ready, you may go on to Capítulo 26 to find out
if little Enrique listens to the diabolical voice!

NOTAS

CAPÍTULO VEINTISÉIS 26

La tormenta nos ha encontrado. Estamos empapados hasta los huesos.
Los rayos me parecen estrechas líneas entre
la vida y la muerte. Pero aún peor, esta presencia satánica
parece penetrar cada gota de agua, cada trueno.
¿Vamos a salir de esto alguna vez?
« ¡Enrique! ¡Creo que tengo razón!
¡Tú debes hacer que la puerta retorcida se abra!
¡Tienes que hacerlo solo, sin mi ayuda!
¡No debes escuchar a este ser maligno! ».
Enrique cierra los ojos. Lo veo morderse el labio inferior.
Entonces, traga saliva. Respira hondo y con un cierto grado
de valor comienza a hacer lo que debe para salvarse.

⬧

The storm has found us. We are soaked to the bone (skin).
The streaks of lightning look to me like narrow lines between
life and death. But even worse, this satanical presence
seems to penetrate each drop of water, each clap of thunder.
Are we ever going to get out of this?
« Enrique! I believe that I am right!
You must make the twisted door open!
You have to do it on your own without my help!
You mustn't listen to this evil being! »
Enrique closes his eyes. I see him bite his lower lip.
Then he swallows hard. He takes a deep breath, and with a certain degree
of courage, he commences to do what he must in order to save himself.

⬧

estar empapado hasta los huesos = to be soaked to the bone (skin)
empapar = to soak; to drench
hasta = as far as; up to
estrecha = narrow (feminine)
una **líne**a = a **line**
entre = between
la **vi**da = the life (think: **vi**able)
peor = worse
cada = each
el agua = the water
vamos = we go
* ir = to go
alguna vez = ever
* **alguna** = any

* **vez** = time
deber = must
cierra = he closes
morder = to bite
tragar = to swallow
respirar hondo = to take a deep breath
hondo = deep

Now you must learn the **to go** verb **ir**.
It is an **-ir** verb but not what you would expect.
That's why it is called an irregular verb!

Here goes:

ir = to go

yo voy = I go; I am going; I do go
tú vas = you go; you are going; you do go
usted va = you go; you are going; you do go
él, ella va = he, she, it goes; he is going; he does go
nosotros, nosotras vamos = we go; we are going; we do go
ustedes van = you go; you are going; you do go
ellos, ellas van = they go; they are going; they do go

Make the effort to learn this verb. You
might need it later. Get my drift?

Now you **must** conjugate the regular **-er** verb **deber**.
No hints! When you have finished, take this test.
Watch out. It's tricky!

1. he does go = _____
2. ir = _____
3. tú debes = _____
4. each = _____
5. water = _____
6. between = _____
7. I go = _____
8. ever = _____
9. he must = _____
10. you (singular) go = _____ or _____
11. yo debo = _____
12. they do go = _____
13. the life = _____

Aquí están las respuestas:

deb**er** = must

yo deb**o** = I must
tú deb**es** = you must
usted deb**e** = you must
él, ella deb**e** = he, she, it must
nosotros, nosotras deb**emos** = we must
ustedes deb**en** = you must
ellos, ellas deb**en** = they must

1. él va
2. to go
3. you must
4. cada
5. agua
6. entre
7. yo voy
8. alguna vez
9. él debe
10. tú vas or usted va
11. I must
12. ellos van or ellas van
13. la vida

If you missed more than one, study and take
the test over if you want to find out what poor Enrique
will do in the next chapter. Will he save himself? When
you are ready, you may proceed to Capítulo 27.

Enrique trata de secar sus ojos mojados por la lluvia,
pero es una batalla perdida.
La lluvia torrencial continúa a pesar de sus esfuerzos.
En efecto, todo parece perdido.
Él se arrodilla frente a la pequeña puerta retorcida.
El lodo cubre sus pequeñas rodillas.
Con un aire de tristeza, me mira como por última vez.
Simulo una sonrisa para darle valor.
Entonces, comienza a decir en voz alta:

« ser = to be
yo soy = I am
tú. . . tú. . . ».

« **¡Me olvidé, Francisca!** ».
« **¡Tú puedes hacerlo, Enrique! ¡Piensa!** ».
El tiempo parece una eternidad. ¡Pero Enrique no parece
recordar!
¿Será condenado por el resto de su vida?
La velocidad del viento aumenta súbitamente.
Hay otra ráfaga de viento muy intensa
acompañada de un rugido petrificante:

« ¡eres. . . eres. . . **eres!** ».

Enrique grita:
« **AHORA LO ENTIENDO:**

¡tú **eres** = you are
usted es = you are
él es = he is
ella es = she is
nosotros somos = we are
nosotras somos = we are
ustedes son = you are
ellos son = they are
ellas son = they are! ».

La minúscula puerta retorcida se abre
por sí misma.

Enrique tries to wipe his eyes moistened by the rain,
but it is a losing battle.
The torrential rain continues despite his efforts.
Indeed, everything seems lost.
He kneels down in front of the little twisted door.
Mud covers his little knees.
With an air of sadness, he looks at me as if for the last time.
I feign a smile in order to give him courage.
Then he begins to say aloud:

« to be = ser
I am = yo soy
you . . . you . . . »

*« **I forgot, Francisca!** »*
*« **You can do it, Enrique! Think!** »*
Time seems an eternity. But Enrique does not look like
he remembers!
Will he be condemned for the rest of his life?
The speed of the wind suddenly increases.
There is another very intense gust of wind
accompanied by a petrifying howl,

*« are . . . are . . . **are!** »*

Enrique screams out,
*« **NOW I GET IT:***

*you **are** = tú eres*
you are = usted es
he is = él es
she is = ella es
we are = nosotros somos
we are = nosotras somos
you are = ustedes son
they are = ellos son
they are = ellas son! »

The tiny twisted door opens
by itself.

tratar de = to try to
secar = to wipe; to dry
la lluvia = the rain
una **bat**alla = a **bat**tle
perdida = lost (feminine)
un **esfu**erzo = an **eff**ort
todo = all; everything (masculine)
el lodo = the mud
como = like; as (if)
última = last (feminine)
una sonrisa = a smile
dar**le** = to give **him**; to give **her**; to give **you** (singular, polite)
* dar = to give
en voz alta = aloud
el **tiem**po = the **tim**e; the weather
la **vi**da = the life (think: **vi**tal)
aumentar = to increase (think: **augment**)
súbitamente = suddenly
muy = very
un rugido = a howl

Now, try learning these indirect object pronouns:
me; **te**; **le**; **nos**; **les**

me = me
te = you (singular, familiar)
le = him; her; you (singular, polite)
nos = us
les = you (plural); them

Here are examples using the **to write** verb **escribir**. (See Capítulo 12.)
Notice that *letter* is the *direct object* of the verb **escribir**.

él **me** escribe una carta = he writes **me** a letter *or* he writes a letter to **me**
yo **te** escribo una carta = I write **you** a letter *or* I write a letter to **you**
yo **le** escribo una carta = I write **him, her,** or **you** a letter *or* I write a letter to
   him, to **her**, or to **you**
ella **nos** escribe una carta = she writes **us** a letter *or* she writes a letter to **us**
yo **les** escribo una carta = I write **you** or **them** a letter *or* I write a letter to **you**
   or to **them**

Did you notice that these indirect object
pronouns are placed *before* the verb **escribir**?

Now study and take this test.

1. to give = _____
2. the battle = _____
3. all = _____
4. like; as = _____
5. the life = _____
6. a smile = _____
7. the time; the weather = _____
8. the rain = _____
9. I write her a letter = _____
10. I write them a letter = _____
11. she writes me a letter = _____
12. I write a letter to you (singular, familiar) = _____
13. he writes a letter to us = _____
14. I write you (plural) a letter = _____
15. I write a letter to him = _____

Aquí están las respuestas:

1. dar
2. la batalla
3. todo
4. como
5. la vida
6. una sonrisa
7. el tiempo
8. la lluvia
9. yo le escribo una carta
10. yo les escribo una carta
11. ella me escribe una carta
12. yo te escribo una carta
13. él nos escribe una carta
14. yo les escribo una carta
15. yo le escribo una carta

If you missed more than one, you cannot go
on to the next chapter. Study and take the test
again if you want to find out in Capítulo 28 what
happens when the little twisted door opens!

Tan pronto como la pequeña puerta se abre, sentimos
un terremoto tan fuerte que nos hace perder el equilibrio.
¡Splash!
Nos encontramos en el suelo completamente cubiertos de lodo.
Enrique trata de levantarse, pero se resbala y termina en el lodo otra vez.
Los temblores cesan.
Entonces, trato de pararme cuando veo algo extraño:
el aire se espesa de forma sobrenatural frente a mí.
Al principio, puedo distinguir algo borroso y grisáceo.
Luego, toma forma.
¡Horrorizada, me doy cuenta que es un ser siniestro que se está formando!
Lo reconozco. . . ¡Es el viejo quien se está materializando!
Entonces, es verdad. ¡El viejo es un fantasma!
Por lo tanto, surge la pregunta obligatoria:
¿por qué se siente obligado a revelarnos su secreto?

*As soon as the little door opens, we feel
such a strong earthquake that it makes us lose our balance.
Splash!
We find ourselves on the ground completely covered in mud.
Enrique tries to get up but he slips and ends up again in the mud.
The tremors cease.
Then, I try to stand up when I see something strange:
the air thickens in an unearthly way in front of me.
At first, I can make out something hazy and grayish.
Then, it takes shape.
Horrified, I realize that it is a sinister being that is forming!
I recognize him . . . It is the old man who is materializing!*

Then, it is true. The old man is a ghost!
Therefore, the obligatory question arises:
why does he feel obligated to reveal his secret to us?

tan pronto como = as soon as
el **terr**emoto = the earthquake
* la **tierr**a = the earth (think: extra**terr**estrial; **terr**ain)
perder = to lose
en el suelo = on the ground
levantarse = to get up
resbalar = to slip
cuando = when
espesar = to thicken
al principio = at first
borroso = blurred; hazy (masculine)
gris**áceo** = gray**ish** (masculine)
* gris = gray
tomar = to take
la forma = the way; the shape
ser = being
reconocer = to **recog**nize
es verdad = it is true
* la verdad = the truth
* es **fals**o = it is **fals**e
* **fals**o = **fals**e
por lo tanto = therefore
la pregunta = the question
por qué = why
* porque = because

Do you remember the endings for **-ar** verbs?
You should! They are **-o**, **-as**, **-a**, **-amos**, **-an**. Now
try to conjugate **tomar** and then take this test.

1. borroso = _____
2. on the ground = _____
3. it is true = _____
4. al principio = _____
5. tomar = _____
6. la verdad = _____
7. to slip = _____
8. grayish = _____

9. to recognize = _____

10. it is false = _____

11. why = _____

12. therefore = _____

Aquí están las respuestas:

tom**ar** = to take

yo tom**o** = I take; I am taking; I do take

tú tom**as** = you take; you are taking; you do take

usted tom**a** = you take; you are taking; you do take

él, ella, tom**a** = he, she, it takes; he is taking; he does take

nosotros, nosotras tom**amos** = we take; we are taking; we do take

ustedes tom**an** = you take; you are taking; you do take

ellos, ellas tom**an** = they take; they are taking; they do take

1. blurred; hazy
2. en el suelo
3. es verdad
4. at first
5. to take
6. the truth
7. resbalar
8. grisáceo
9. reconocer
10. es falso
11. por qué
12. por lo tanto

If you missed more than two, study and take the test over. Then when you are ready, you may go on to Capítulo 29 to find out what the phantom is up to!

NOTAS

Los pequeños ojos negros del fantasma se concentran en el pequeño Enrique.
Con una sarcástica sonrisa, y con
una resonante voz aún más grave, el viejo profetiza:

« ¡Ah! ¡Enrique, di adiós a Francisca!
¡Dame la mano! ».

« ¡No, Enrique! ¡No lo escuches! ¡Debo de estar sobre
la pista correcta! **¡Por eso él se ha materializado!** ».
Oigo un gruñido espantoso.
« ¡Enrique, toca la pequeña puerta retorcida! ».
Los terremotos comienzan otra vez,
¡pero el fantasma es engañado porque sus trucos no funcionan tan
bien **sobre sujetos que ya están en el suelo!**
Enrique se aprovecha de la situación:
todavía tendido en el suelo, toca la pequeña puerta
con una mano y extiende la otra hacia mí.
Yo reacciono muy rápidamente dándole la mano.
Por un instante formamos los eslabones de una cadena humana.
Levanto la cabeza para dar una última mirada al
cielo tormentoso y grito:
« ¡Gracias, Viento! ».
Y la tormenta inmediatamente cesa.

The little black eyes of the phantom concentrate on little Enrique.
With a sarcastic smile, and with
an even lower resonant voice, the old man prophesies,

« ***Ah! Enrique, say farewell to Francisca!***
Give me your hand! »

« *No, Enrique! Don't listen to him! I must be on*
the right track! **That's why he has materialized!** »
I hear a dreadful growl.
« *Enrique, touch the little twisted door!* »
The earthquakes start all over again,
but the phantom is fooled because his tricks don't work as
well **on subjects that are already on the ground!**
Enrique takes advantage of the situation:
still lying on the ground, he touches the little door
with one hand and extends the other one toward me.
I react very quickly by giving him my hand.
For an instant we form the links of a human chain.
I raise my head up in order to get one last look at the
stormy sky and I scream,
« *Thank you, Wind!* »
And the storm immediately stops.

⬚

una son**ris**a = a smile
* un **ris**a = a laugh
re**son**ante = resonant (think: **soun**d)
* el **son**ido = the **soun**d
da**me** = give **me**
* dar = to give
la pista = the track
por eso = that's why
un gruñido = a growl
espantoso = dreadful (masculine)
otra vez = again; (all over) again
* otra = another (feminine)
* vez = time
un **tru**co = a **tric**k
los **sujet**os = the **subject**s
ya = already
se aprovecha de = he takes advantage of
* aprovecharse de = to take advantage of
rápida**mente** = quick**ly**; fast
un eslabón = a link
el cielo = the sky; the heaven
tormentoso = stormy (masculine)
gracias = thank you

Now learn how to conjugate the **to give** verb, **dar**.
It is irregular so watch out!

d**ar** = to give

yo doy = I give; I am giving; I do give
tú d**as** = you give; you are giving; you do give
usted d**a** = you give; you are giving; you do give
él, ella d**a** = he, she, it gives; he is giving; he does give
nosotros, nosotras d**amos** = we give; we are giving; we do give
ustedes d**an** = you give; you are giving; you do give
ellos, ellas d**an** = they give; they are giving; they do give

Now take this test.

1. un eslabón = _____
2. that's why = _____
3. the sound = _____
4. a smile = _____
5. a laugh = _____
6. ya = _____
7. I give = _____
8. the sky = _____
9. again = _____
10. he gives = _____
11. un gruñido = _____
12. thank you = _____

Aquí están las respuestas:

1. a link
2. por eso
3. el sonido
4. una sonrisa
5. una risa
6. already
7. yo doy
8. el cielo
9. otra vez
10. él da
11. a growl
12. gracias

If you missed more than one, study and
take the test over if you want to find out what
awaits Enrique and Francisca in Capítulo 30!

NOTAS

¡Pum!
¡Nos encontramos sobre el piso en la habitación de la pintura viviente!
¡Logramos salir del cementerio!
Nos levantamos lentamente.
A pesar de la conmoción,
somos inmediatamente atraídos hacia la pintura viviente.
Enrique se para frente a mí para estudiar la pintura más de cerca.
« Nada ha cambiado, Francisca, las puertas retorcidas están
todavía allí », dice con un aire de decepción.
A su vez, yo analizo la pintura. . .
Me temo que el pobre Enrique tiene razón.
Entonces noto algo.
« Enrique, dale otra mirada a esta pintura al óleo. ¿Qué ves tú? ».
« Yo veo unas puertas retorcidas ».
« Ahora, dime qué **no ves** ».
Me mira perplejo.
Él reexamina la pintura. Luego, lo veo saltar por el aire.
« ¡No estoy allí! ¡Ya no estoy allí! ».
« ¡Liberamos tu espíritu, Enrique! », grito con todas mis fuerzas.
¡Los dos saltamos de alegría
mientras hacemos un alboroto increíble!
« ¡Shhh. . . ! ».
« ¿Tú dijiste eso, Enrique? ».
« Nooooo », responde muy preocupado.
« Creí que habías sido tú, Francisca ».
« No, no fui yo ».

Thud!
We find ourselves on the ground in the room with the living painting!
We succeeded in getting out of the cemetery!
We get up slowly.
In spite of the shock,
we are immediately drawn to the living painting.
Enrique stands in front of me in order to study the painting more closely.
« Nothing has changed, Francisca, the twisted doors are
still there, » he says with a look of disappointment.
In turn, I analyze the picture . . .
I fear that poor Enrique is right.
Then I notice something.
« Enrique, give this oil painting another look. What do you see? »
« I see some twisted doors. »
*« Now, tell me what **you don't see**. »*
He looks at me perplexed.
He re-examines the painting. Then, I see him jump up in the air.
« I am not there! I am no longer there! »
« We freed your spirit, Enrique! » I shout at the top of my voice.
We both jump for joy
while we make an unbelievable racket!
« Shhh . . . ! »
« Did you say that, Enrique? »
« Nooooo, » he answers very worried.
« I thought that it was you, Francisca. »
« No, it wasn't me. »

¡pum! = thud!; bang!
lograr = to succeed
levantarse = to get up
la conmoción = the shock
inmediata**mente** = immediate**ly**
e**stud**iar = to **stud**y
nada = nothing
todavía = still; yet
la decepción = the disappointment
a su vez = in turn
notar = to **not**ice
da**le** = give **it**
pintura al óleo = oil **paint**ing
óleo = oil (painting)
ahora = now
di**me** = tell **me**
luego = afterwards; then
saltar = to jump
alegría = joy

Now you must learn how to say the following:

I give; **I do not give**; **I never give**;
I give nothing; **I do not give any more**;
I do not give anything else; **I always give**;
I give everything; **I always give everything**

Remember in Capítulo 8 you learned to put
no in front of the verb to make it negative?
This is very similar. Watch this!

yo doy = I give

no = not
yo **no** doy = I do **not** give

nunca = never; ever
no. . . **nunca** = never; not ever
yo **no** doy **nunca** = I **never** give or I do **not ever** give

nada = nothing
no. . . **nada** = nothing; not anything
yo **no** doy **nada** = I give **nothing** or I do **not** give **anything**

más = more
no. . . **más** = not . . . any more
yo **no** doy **más** = I do **not** give **any more**

no. . . **nada más** = not . . . anything else
yo **no** doy **nada más** = I do **not** give **anything else**

siempre = always
yo **siempre** doy = I **always** give

todo = everything
yo doy **todo** = I give **everything**

siempre. . . **todo** = always . . . everything
yo **siempre** doy **todo** = I **always** give **everything**

Get it? You had better look it over
before this little test. However, you might really
need it later for a much more important reason!

Now take this test.

1. nothing = _____
2. más = _____
3. to succeed = _____
4. you (singular, familiar) never give = _____
5. alegría = _____
6. inmediatamente = _____
7. I give everything = _____
8. you (singular, polite) give nothing = _____
9. to study = _____
10. now = _____
11. usted siempre da todo = _____
12. always = _____
13. to get up = _____
14. pintura al óleo = _____
15. saltar = _____
16. afterwards = _____

Aquí están las respuestas:

1. nada
2. more
3. lograr
4. tú no das nunca
5. joy
6. immediately
7. yo doy todo
8. usted no da nada
9. estudiar
10. ahora
11. you always give everything
12. siempre
13. levantarse
14. oil painting
15. to jump
16. luego

If you missed more than two, study and take
the test over. Be well prepared. This is a warning!
When you are ready, you may go on to Capítulo 31.

« ¿Si no fuiste tú, y no fui yo, entonces quién dijo 'shhh'? ».

« Yo no sé.

Sólo estamos tú, yo y esta pintura en la habitación ».

« Bueno, probablemente es algún sonido sin ningún significado.

Todas estas casas viejas tienen pequeños ruidos de crujidos y chirridos,

¿no es así, Enrique? ».

« No ».

« ¿Por qué dijiste 'no'? ».

« Yo no dije 'no' ».

« ¿Cómo que no dijiste 'no'? ».

« Te estoy diciendo que no dije 'no' ».

« Enrique. Éste no es momento para burlarte de mí ».

« Yo no estoy burlándome de ti ».

« Sí lo estás. Estoy empezando a enojarme ».

« ¿Por qué te estás enojando? Yo no hice nada ».

« Sí lo hiciste. Estás diciendo que no dijiste 'no' ».

« Yo no dije 'no' ».

« ¿Cómo que no dijiste 'no'? ».

« Te estoy diciendo que no. . . ».

« ¡Paren! ».

« ¿Quién dijo eso? ».

« Yo no ».

« ¡Ohhhh, no vamos a empezar esto otra vez! ».

« ¡Eso es verdad! », *dice la pintura.*

⬚

« If it wasn't you, and it wasn't me, then who said 'shhh'? »
« I don't know.
There's only you, me, and this painting in the room. »
« All right, it's probably some sound without any significance.
All these old houses have little noises of creaking(s) and squeaking(s),
don't they, Enrique? »
« No. »
« Why did you say 'no'? »
« I didn't say 'no.' »
« What do you mean you didn't say 'no'? »
« I'm telling you that I did not say 'no.' »
« Enrique. This is no time to mock me. »
« I'm not mocking you. »
« Yes, you are. I'm starting to get mad. »
« Why are you getting mad? I didn't do anything. »
« Yes, you did. You are saying that you did not say 'no.' »
« I didn't say 'no.' »

« What do you mean you didn't say 'no'? »
« I'm telling you that I did not . . . »
« Stop! »
« Who said that? »
« Not me. »
« Ohhhh, we're not going to start this all over again! »
« That's true! » says the painting.

◈

¿quién? = who?
* decir = to say; to tell
(yo) no sé = I don't know
la habitación = the room
bueno = all right; good (masculine)
* el día = the day
* buenos días = good morning
algún = some
el sonido = the sound
sin = without
el significado = the meaning; the significance
el ruido = the noise
un crujido = a creaking
un chirrido = a squeaking
¿no es así? = isn't that so?
enojarse = to get mad
parar = to stop

◈

You are going to learn **to say** the verb **decir**.
It is irregular. Watch out for the **yo** form!

dec**ir** = to say; to tell

yo dig**o** = I say; I am saying; I do say
tú dic**es** = you say; you are saying; you do say
usted dic**e** = you say; you are saying; you do say
él, ella dic**e** = he, she, it says; he is saying; he does say
nosotros, nosotras dec**imos** = we say; we are saying; we do say
ustedes dic**en** = you say; you are saying; you do say
ellos, ellas dic**en** = they say; they are saying; they do say

Now you need to learn how to say **I have said**.

I have said is **yo he dicho**. This compound tense (so-called because it conjugates with a helping verb) is called the *pretérito perfecto* or the present perfect indicative in English. You are going to learn the *pretérito perfecto* because it is commonly used in Spanish and yet it is far less complicated to learn than the past preterite tense called the *pretérito*. In this chapter, yo **dije** or I **did say** is an example of the *pretérito*. To form the *pretérito perfecto*, all you do is conjugate the present indicative of the helping verb **haber** (**to have**) and then add a past participle which in this case is **dicho**. Study the conjugation of the *pretérito perfecto* of **decir**:

decir = to say

yo **he** dicho = I **have** said
tú **has** dicho = you **have** said
usted **ha** dicho = you **have** said
él, ella **ha** dicho = he, she **has** said
nosotros, nosotras **hemos** dicho = we **have** said
ustedes **han** dicho = you **have** said
ellos, ellas **han** dicho = they **have** said

Clear? Now study the conjugation of the helping verb **haber** which is in bold letters. Then take this little test. Hint: No tricks. The whole test will be about **to have said**.

1. you (singular) have said = _____ or _____
2. he has said = _____
3. yo he dicho = _____
4. we have said = _____ or _____
5. ellos han dicho = _____
6. you (plural) have said = _____
7. she has said = _____
8. I have said = _____

Aquí están las respuestas:

1. tú has dicho or usted ha dicho
2. él ha dicho
3. I have said
4. nosotros hemos dicho or nosotras hemos dicho
5. they have said
6. ustedes han dicho
7. ella ha dicho
8. yo he dicho

Ready for one more complication?
What if you want to say, **I have not said**.
You are going to put the **no** before the helping verb **haber**.
The past participle **dicho** is not touched! Watch this:

yo **no** he dicho = I have not said
tú **no** has dicho = you have not said
usted **no** ha dicho = you have not said
él, ella **no** ha dicho = he, she has not said
nosotros, nosotras **no** hemos dicho = we have not said
ustedes **no** han dicho = you have not said
ellos, ellas **no** han dicho = they have not said

You have seen that it is not too difficult to form the *pretérito perfecto* once you know the past participle that you must use.
So, here are the general rules for forming the *pretérito perfecto* and determining the past participle for **-ar**, **-er**, and **-ir** verbs:
First, you conjugate the present indicative of the helping verb **haber** and then add the past participle which is formed in the following way:

For **-ar** verbs, take the **root** of the infinitive (**cont**ar) and add **ado**.
So, the past participle is **contado**.
Example: we have counted = nosotros hemos cont**ado**

For **-er** verbs, take the **root** of the infinitive (**entend**er) and add **ido**.
So, the past participle is **entendido**.
Example: they have understood = ellos han entend**ido**

For **-ir** verbs, take the **root** of the infinitive (**viv**ir) and add **ido**.
So, the past participle is **vivido**.
Example: you have lived = tú has viv**ido**

But beware!
You will encounter verbs like **decir**
that do not obey these exact rules!

Now, instead of a big test, go back and study the
conjugation of **haber** along with the rules for forming
past participles. Believe me, you may need to know
all this later! When you feel very secure about
knowing these, go on to Capítulo 32!

¡Esta pintura verdaderamente ha hablado!
Nos miramos.
« ¡Ah! », grita Enrique.
Los dos corremos hacia la puerta para escaparnos de
la pintura parlante cuando oímos:

En la casa están las puertas retorcidas,
Pasen por ellas para escapar.
Pero, mis niños:
¡Las apariencias engañan!
Estas puertas son muy difíciles de encontrar.

La voz dulce, pero resuelta, de la pintura
me tranquiliza. Quizás esté equivocada, pero tengo la
impresión de que no representa ningún peligro para nosotros.
« Enrique, espera. Yo no creo que esta pintura
sea maligna. Al contrario, tengo la impresión de
que quiere ayudarnos. ¿Has escuchado lo que ha dicho?
¡Tenemos que pasar por las puertas retorcidas para
escapar de la casa! ».
Enrique todavía no está convencido. Él permanece pegado
a la puerta de salida.
« Yo me quedo acá. Uno nunca sabe. Uno tiene que tomar
precauciones », dice con una voz débil.
« Además, ¡no hay puertas retorcidas en la
casa, excepto en el cementerio y en la *pintura misma!*
¡Esta pintura parlante es quizás una treta del fantasma! ».
« Escucha, Enrique. Yo también estoy asustada, pero no tenemos otra opción.
¡La pintura es nuestro único recurso! ».
Enrique suspira.
« De acuerdo. Supongamos que esto no es un truco
del fantasma y que existen las puertas retorcidas
en la casa. ¿Cómo podemos encontrarlas? ».
Enrique me mira con un aire de ironía:
« ¡Podemos preguntarle al fantasma! ».
« ¡A veces me irritas! Sin embargo, tu idea no es
tan tonta después de todo ».
« ¿Qué quieres decir Francisca? », dice perplejo.
« ¡Podemos preguntarle a la pintura! ».
Sin esperar la respuesta de Enrique (yo creo que
es mejor así), camino hacia la pintura al óleo.
« Pintura bonita, ¿dónde están las puertas retorcidas? ».
Me sobresalto cuando me responde:

¡Las puertas retorcidas las vas a encontrar
Dónde no te atreverías a entrar!

This painting has really spoken!
We look at each other.
« Ah! » cries out Enrique.
We both run toward the door to escape from
the talking painting when we hear:

In the house are the twisted doors,
Go through them to escape.
But, my children:
Appearances deceive!
These doors are very difficult to find.

The sweet but resolute voice of the painting
puts my mind at ease. Perhaps I am wrong, but I have the
impression that it doesn't pose any danger to us.
« Enrique, wait. I don't believe that this painting
is evil. On the contrary, I have the impression
that it wants to help us. Have you heard what it has said?
We have to go through the twisted doors in order
to escape from the house! *»*
Enrique is still not convinced. He stays glued
to the exit door.
« I'm staying here. One never knows. One has to take
precautions, » he says with a feeble voice.
« Besides, there are no twisted doors in the
house except in the cemetery and in the painting itself!
This talking painting is perhaps a trick by the phantom! »
« Listen, Enrique. I'm scared too, but we have no other choice.
The painting is our only recourse! »
Enrique sighs.
« O.K. Let's suppose that this isn't a trick
by the phantom and that the twisted doors exist
in the house. How can we find them? »
Enrique looks at me with an air of irony:
« We can (always) ask the phantom! »
« Sometimes you irritate me! However, your idea is not
so foolish after all. »
« What do you mean, Francisca? » he says perplexed.
« We can ask the painting! »
Without waiting for Enrique's answer (I believe that
it is better this way), I walk toward the oil painting.
« Pretty painting, where are the twisted doors? »
I jump when it answers me:

The twisted doors you are going to find
Where you would not dare enter!

hablar = to speak; to talk
parlante = talking
pasar por = to go through
dulce = sweet (feminine and masculine)
quizás = perhaps
tener la **impresión** de que = to have the **impression** that
creo = I believe
* creer = to believe
al **contrar**io = on the **contrar**y
escuchado = heard
tenemos que pasar por = we have to go through
* tener que = to have to
permanecer = to stay
quedarse = to stay
acá = here
nunca = never
además = besides; moreover
no hay = there is **not**; there are **not**
* hay = there is; there are
una **tr**eta = a **tr**ick; a ruse
suspirar = to sigh
de acuerdo = all right; O.K.; agreed
encontrar**las** = to find **them**
preguntar = to ask
a veces = sometimes
tonta = foolish; silly (feminine)
querer decir = to mean
mejor = better
así = thus; in this way
bonita = pretty (feminine)
atreverse = to dare

How do you think you would conjugate the
pretérito perfecto of **hablar**? Do you remember how
to form the past participle for **-ar** verbs? No hints.
Try it yourself now.

How do think you would say, **I have not spoken**?

How would you say, **I have not spoken any more**?

Now study and take this test!

1. sweet = _____
2. suspirar = _____
3. así = _____
4. creer = _____
5. además = _____
6. una treta = _____
7. no hay = _____
8. on the contrary = _____
9. foolish (masculine) = _____
10. foolish (feminine) = _____
11. I have to believe = _____
12. bonita = _____
13. I have the impression that = _____
14. you (singular, familiar) have the impression that = _____
15. to stay = _____ or _____
16. de acuerdo = _____

Aquí están las respuestas:

yo **he** hablado = I **have** spoken
tú **has** hablado = you **have** spoken
usted **ha** hablado = you **have** spoken
él, ella **ha** hablado = he, she **has** spoken
nosotros **hemos** hablado = we **have** spoken
ustedes **han** hablado = you **have** spoken
ellos, ellas **han** hablado = they **have** spoken

I have **not** spoken = yo **no** he hablado
I have **not** spoken **any more** = yo **no** he hablado **más**

1. dulce
2. to sigh
3. thus
4. to believe
5. besides; moreover
6. a trick; a ruse
7. there is not; there are not
8. al contrario
9. tonto
10. tonta
11. yo tengo que creer
12. pretty
13. yo tengo la impresión de que
14. tú tienes la impresión de que
15. permanecer; quedarse
16. O.K.; all right; agreed

If you missed more than three, study and take the
entire test over. If you need to, slow down and take
your time. It is always better to do a good job slowly
than a bad job quickly! Your work will pay off later,
if you get my meaning! When you are ready to find
out what the speaking painting's riddles mean,
you may go on to Capítulo 33.

NOTAS

¡Yo no esperaba que la pintura me contestara!
Trato de calmarme.
Todavía sin aliento, repito las adivinanzas:

Las apariencias engañan

**Las puertas retorcidas las vas a encontrar
Dónde no te atreverías a entrar**

« Éstas son adivinanzas, Enrique. Yo no entiendo nada ».
Enrique no me responde mientras abre muy suavemente la puerta
de la habitación. Él echa un vistazo desde el umbral de la puerta.
Nadie. El pasillo está vacío.
Entramos y nos encontramos con un pasillo muy extraño.
Hay sombras y luces que parecen danzar
por las paredes y las puertas de madera.
Pero hay algo ilógico:
no hay una fuente aparente para
estas luces que saltan alrededor.
Súbitamente, las luces cesan su danza. Entonces,
se apagan. El pasillo se ennegrece y se llena de una
terrible y horrorosa presencia.
« ¡Ah, allí están, niños! »,
resuena su voz como un trueno.
« ¡Apresúrate, Enrique, corre! ¡Sálvate!
¡Empuja la puerta de madera que está frente a ti! ».
Pero el pequeño Enrique se da la vuelta para enfrentar a su enemigo. . .
¡Comienza a correr, no hacia la puerta de madera para salvarse,

sino hacia la presencia misma!
« ¡No, Enrique! ¡Para! », grito con todas mis fuerzas.
Pero él persiste en correr hacia el peligro mortal.
« ¡Estás presenciando tus últimas horas! »,
exclama el espectro.
Entonces, oigo un espantoso grito. Silencio.
« ¡Enrique! ¡Enrique! ¿Qué has hecho, mi pobre Enrique? ».
Sin pensar, yo misma me encuentro corriendo hacia
el ser maligno.
Aunque muera, debo tratar de salvar al pequeño Enrique.
Veo la gran presencia frente a mí.
Es negruzca y parece llenar todo el pasillo.
Cierro los ojos y salto hacia ella. . .

I wasn't expecting that the painting would answer me!
I try to calm myself.
Still out of breath, I repeat the riddles:

Appearances deceive

The twisted doors you are going to find
Where you would not dare enter

« These are riddles, Enrique. I don't understand a thing. »
Enrique doesn't answer me while very gently opening the door
to the room. He casts a glance through the doorway.
Nobody. The hall is empty.
We enter and we find a very strange hallway.
There are shadows and lights that seem to dance
along the walls and wooden doors.
But there is something illogical:
there is no apparent source for
these lights that jump about.
Suddenly, the lights cease their dance. Then,
they go out. The hall blackens and fills with a
terrible and horrifying presence.
« Ah, you are there, children! »
his voice resonates like a clap of thunder.
« Hurry, Enrique, run! Save yourself!
Push on the wooden door that is in front of you! »
But little Enrique turns around to face his enemy . . .
He starts to run, not toward the wooden door to save himself,

but toward the presence itself!
« No, Enrique! Stop! » I yell at the top of my voice.
But he persists in running toward mortal danger.
« You are witnessing your last hours! »
exclaims the specter.
Then, I hear a dreadful cry. Silence.
« Enrique! Enrique! What have you done, my poor Enrique? »
Without thinking, I find myself running toward
the evil being.
Even if I die, I must try to save little Enrique.
I see the large presence in front of me.
It is blackish and seems to fill the entire hallway.
I close my eyes and I jump toward it . . .

esperar = to expect; to wait (for)
calmar**me** = to calm **myself**
una **adivin**anza = a riddle
* **adivin**ar = to guess
entender = to understand
echar un vistazo = to cast a glance; to have a quick look at
nadie = nobody
un pasillo = a hall(way) (US); a corridor
vacío = empty (masculine) (think: **vac**ant)
una sombra = a shadow
las luces = the lights
una pared = a wall
saltar = to jump
ennegrecer = to black**en**
* negro = black
llenar = to fill
apresurarse = to hurry
darse la vuelta = to turn around
un **enem**igo = an **enem**y
un peligro = a danger
aunque = even if
tratar de = to try to
negr**uzco** = black**ish** (masculine)

Now learn how to conjugate the verb **entender**.
It is an **-er** verb. But notice how the letter **i** has
to be inserted in all of the conjugations
except for the **nosotros** form.

entend**er** = to understand

yo entiend**o** = I understand; I do understand
tú entiend**es** = you understand; you do understand
usted entiend**e** = you understand; you do understand
él, ella entiend**e** = he, she, it understands; he does understand
nosotros, nosotras entend**emos** = we understand; we do understand
ustedes entiend**en** = you understand; you do understand
ellos, ellas entiend**en** = they understand; they do understand

If **hecho** means **done** and is the past participle of
the **to do** verb **hacer**, how do you think you would
conjugate the *pretérito perfecto* of this verb?

What are the past participles of the verbs
trat**ar**, corr**er**, and repet**ir**? No hints! Answer these
questions now and then take the test below.

1. a riddle = _____
2. ennegrecer = _____
3. you (plural) do understand = _____
4. echar un vistazo = _____
5. we understand = _____
6. I do understand = _____
7. empty = _____
8. a hall = _____
9. she understands = _____
10. to try to = _____
11. llenar = _____
12. blackish = _____
13. we do understand = _____
14. a wall = _____
15. they understand = _____
16. darse la vuelta = _____

Aquí están las respuestas:

yo **he** hecho = I **have** done
tú **has** hecho = you **have** done
usted **ha** hecho = you **have** done
él, ella **ha** hecho = he, she, it **has** done
nosotros, nosotras **hemos** hecho = we **have** done
ustedes **han** hecho = you **have** done
ellos, ellas **han** hecho = they **have** done

The past participle of trat**ar** is trat**ado**.
The past participle of corr**er** is corr**ido**.
The past participle of repet**ir** is repet**ido**.

1. una adivinanza
2. to blacken
3. ustedes entienden
4. to cast a glance; to have a quick look at
5. nosotros entendemos or nosotras entendemos
6. yo entiendo
7. vacío
8. un pasillo
9. ella entiende
10. tratar de
11. to fill
12. negruzco
13. nosotros entendemos or nosotras entendemos
14. una pared
15. ellos entienden or ellas entienden
16. to turn around

Now, if you missed more than two on
the test, study well and take the test over.
Then when you are ready, you may proceed to
Capítulo 34 if you want to find out what the future
holds for Francisca as she tries to save poor Enrique!

Abro los ojos. Estoy respirando. . . Debo de estar viva.
Veo mal. . . Todo está borroso, grisáceo.
Extiendo la mano.
Toco algo suave y tibio.
« ¿Francisca? », él murmura.
« ¿Enrique? ¿Eres tú? ¿Estás bien? ».
El contorno borroso de la cara de Enrique empieza a
enfocarse. Por fin, su cara toma forma.
« ¡Enrique! ¿Estás bien? ¿Qué hiciste? ».
« Yo pensé, Francisca. . . pensé en las adivinanzas ».
« ¿Qué? ».
« Tú siempre me has dicho que piense, ¿no es así? ».
« Sí, pero. . . esto es absurdo. ¡Ahora estamos
atrapados dentro de un fantasma! ».
Enrique parece calmado.
« No, Francisca. Yo no creo que estemos atrapados.
Mira allí, un poco más lejos »,
dice, señalando.
En efecto, *¡es una puerta retorcida!*

I open my eyes. I am breathing . . . I must be alive.
I see poorly . . . Everything is blurred, grayish.
I hold out my hand.
I touch something soft and warm.
« Francisca? » he murmurs.
« Enrique? Is it you? Are you all right? »
The blurry contour of Enrique's face starts to
come into focus. Finally, his face takes shape.
« Enrique! Are you O.K.? What did you do? »
« I thought, Francisca . . . I thought about the riddles. »
« What? »
« You've always told me to think, isn't that so? »
« Yes, but . . . this is absurd. Now we are
trapped inside a ghost! »
Enrique appears calm.
« No, Francisca. I don't believe that we are trapped.
Look over there, a little farther down, »
he says, pointing.
Indeed, it is a twisted door!

abrir = to open
respirar = to breathe (think: **respir**ation)
estar vivo = to be alive (masculine)
* la vida = the life
mal = bad(ly); poorly
suave = soft; mild
tibio = warm
¿(tú) estás bien? = are you O.K.?; are you all right?
* ¿cómo estás? = how are you?
qué = what
¿no es así? = isn't that so?
un poco = a little
más = more
lejos = far
más lejos = farther

Do you remember in Capítulo 2 you learned
how to conjugate the **to be** verb, **estar**?
This same verb is used in the following expression:
How are you?

Watch this:

¿cómo **estás (tú)**? = how **are you**? (singular and familiar)
¿cómo **está (usted)**? = how **are you**? (singular and polite)

The answers to these questions are the following:

estoy muy bien = I am very well
no estoy muy bien = I am not very well

Now review the conjugation of **estar**.
By just adding **muy bien**, a very
fine expression is formed!

(yo) **estoy** muy bien = I am very well
(tú) **estás** muy bien = you are very well
(usted) **está** muy bien = you are very well
(él, ella) **está** muy bien = he, she is very well
(nosotros, nosotras) **estamos** muy bien = we are very well
(ustedes) **están** muy bien = you are very well
(ellos, ellas) **están** muy bien = they are very well

Now take this test.

1. to open = _____
2. warm = _____
3. how are you (singular)? = _____ or _____
4. he is very well = _____
5. isn't that so? = _____
6. they are very well = _____
7. how are you (plural)? = _____
8. I am very well = _____
9. we are not very well = _____
10. far = _____
11. farther = _____
12. a little = _____
13. I am not very well = _____

Aquí están las respuestas:

1. abrir
2. tibio
3. ¿cómo estás (tú)? or ¿cómo está (usted)?
4. él está muy bien
5. ¿no es así?
6. (ellos, ellas) están muy bien
7. ¿cómo están (ustedes)?
8. (yo) estoy muy bien
9. (nosotros, nosotras) no estamos muy bien
10. lejos
11. más lejos
12. un poco
13. (yo) no estoy muy bien

If you missed more than one, study and take the
test over. Then when you are ready, you may go
on to Capítulo 35 to discover the secrets of
the twisted door found inside the ghost!

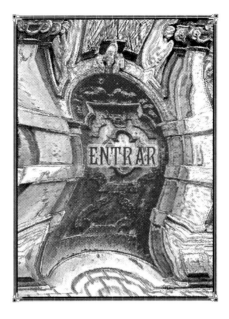

Nos miramos el uno al otro con alegría.
« ¡Enrique, eres un genio! ».
El pequeño Enrique sonríe modestamente.
Caminamos lentamente hacia la puerta retorcida.
Es muy extraña, de madera y grande, con los bordes retorcidos,
al igual que el resto de la puerta. Aun el marco que rodea
la puerta está retorcido. Lógicamente,
no debería existir y sin embargo está aquí, frente a nosotros.
Curiosa, **pongo la mano sobre ella.**
Inmediatamente después, letras doradas rodeadas por un tipo
de halo aparecen en la puerta creando la siguiente palabra:

ENTRAR

We look at one another with joy.
« Enrique, you're a genius! »
Little Enrique smiles modestly.
We walk slowly toward the twisted door.
It is very bizarre, wooden, big, the edges twisted
as well as the rest of the door. Even the frame that surrounds
the door is twisted. Logically,
it should not exist, and yet it is here in front of us.
*Curious, **I place my hand on it.***
***Immediately after,** golden letters surrounded by a type*
of halo appear on the door creating the following words:

TO ENTER

Can you conjugate this verb for Francisca?
You must do it for her if you want to find out what
happens in the next chapter. Deal?

Aquí están las respuestas:

entrar = to enter
yo entro = I enter
tú entras = you enter
usted entra = you enter
él, ella entra = he, she, it enters
nosotros, nosotras entramos = we enter
ustedes entran = you enter
ellos, ellas entran = they enter

If you missed even one, you cannot proceed to the
next chapter and the door will not open for Francisca!
So study until you can fulfill the twisted door's demands!
When you have made no mistakes, you may go
on to Capítulo 36. A little word of warning:
Danger lurks behind one of the doors!

La puerta retorcida se abre por sí misma. . .
« Entremos, Enrique ».
Entramos por la puerta retorcida. Inmediatamente,
se cierra detrás de nosotros con el sonido de una puerta muy pesada.
« ¡Francisca, mira lo que hay frente a nosotros! ».
« ¡Vaya, otra puerta retorcida! ».
Enrique pone su pequeña mano sobre esta nueva puerta retorcida.
Inmediatamente después, letras doradas rodeadas por un tipo
de halo aparecen en la puerta creando las siguientes palabras:

SER

TENER

The twisted door opens by itself . . .
« Let's enter, Enrique. »
We enter by way of the twisted door. Immediately,
it closes behind us with the sound of a very heavy door.
« Francisca, look at what there is in front of us! »
« Well, another twisted door! »
Enrique places his little hand on this new twisted door.
Immediately after, golden letters surrounded by a type
of halo appear on the door creating the following words:

TO BE

TO HAVE

Can you help Enrique conjugate these two verbs?
His fate is in your hands!

Aquí están las respuestas!

ser = to be
yo soy = I am
tú eres = you are
usted es = you are
él, ella es = he, she, it is
nosotros, nosotras somos = we are
ustedes son = you are
ellos, ellas son = they are

tener = to have
yo tengo = I have
tú tienes = you have
usted tiene = you have
él, ella tiene = he, she, it has
nosotros, nosotras tenemos = we have
ustedes tienen = you have
ellos, ellas tienen = they have

If you missed even one, the door
will not open for Enrique! So study until
you can fulfill the twisted door's demands!
When you have made no mistakes, you may go
on to Capítulo 37. A little word of warning:
Danger lurks behind one of the doors!

La puerta retorcida se abre por sí misma. . .
« Entremos, Francisca ».
Entramos por la puerta retorcida. Inmediatamente,
se cierra detrás de nosotros con el sonido de una puerta muy pesada.
« ¡Enrique, mira lo que hay frente a nosotros! ».
« ¡Vaya, otra puerta retorcida! ».
Pongo la mano sobre esta nueva puerta retorcida.
Inmediatamente después, letras doradas rodeadas por un tipo
de halo aparecen en la puerta creando las siguientes palabras:

IR
LLAMARSE
ESTAR
DECIR

The twisted door opens by itself . . .
« Let's enter, Francisca. »
We enter by way of the twisted door. Immediately,
it closes behind us with the sound of a very heavy door.
« Enrique, look at what there is in front of us! »
« Well, another twisted door! »
I place my hand on this new twisted door.
Immediately after, golden letters surrounded by a type
of halo appear on the door creating the following words:

TO GO
TO BE NAMED
TO BE
TO SAY

Can you help Francisca conjugate these verbs?
Her fate is in your hands!

Aquí están las respuestas:

ir = to go
yo voy = I go
tú vas = you go
usted va = you go
él, ella va = he, she, it goes
nosotros, nosotras vamos = we go
ustedes van = you go
ellos, ellas van = they go

llamarse = to be named
yo me llamo = my name is
tú te llamas = your name is
usted se llama = your name is
él, ella se llama = his, her, its name is
nosotros, nosotras nos llamamos = our names are
ustedes se llaman = your names are
ellos, ellas se llaman = their names are

estar = to be
yo estoy = I am
tú estás = you are
usted está = you are
él, ella está = he, she, it is
nosotros, nosotras estamos = we are
ustedes están = you are
ellos, ellas están = they are

decir = to say; to tell
yo digo = I say
tú dices = you say
usted dice = you say
él, ella dice = he, she, it says
nosotros, nosotras decimos = we say
ustedes dicen = you say
ellos, ellas dicen = they say

If you missed even one, the door
will not open for Francisca! So study until
you can fulfill the twisted door's demands!
When you have made no mistakes, you may go
on to Capítulo 38. A little word of warning:
Danger lurks behind one of the doors!

La puerta retorcida se abre por sí misma. . .
« Entremos, Enrique ».
Entramos por la puerta retorcida. Inmediatamente,
se cierra detrás de nosotros con el sonido de una puerta muy pesada.
« ¡Francisca, mira lo que hay frente a nosotros! ».
« ¡Vaya, otra puerta retorcida! ».
Enrique pone su pequeña mano sobre esta nueva puerta retorcida.
Inmediatamente después, letras doradas rodeadas por un tipo
de halo aparecen en la puerta creando las siguientes palabras:

SALIR

VER

DAR

The twisted door opens by itself . . .
« Let's enter, Enrique. »
We enter by way of the twisted door. Immediately,
it closes behind us with the sound of a very heavy door.
« Francisca, look at what there is in front of us! »
« Well, another twisted door! »
Enrique places his little hand on this new twisted door.
Immediately after, golden letters surrounded by a type
of halo appear on the door creating the following words:

TO GO OUT (TO LEAVE)

TO SEE

TO GIVE

Can you help Enrique conjugate these verbs?
His fate is in your hands!

Aquí están las respuestas:

salir = to go out; to leave
yo salgo = I go out
tú sales = you go out
usted sale = you go out
él, ella, sale = he, she, it goes out
nosotros, nosotras salimos = we go out
ustedes salen = you go out
ellos, ellas salen = they go out

ver = to see
yo veo = I see
tú ves = you see
usted ve = you see
él, ella ve = he, she, it sees
nosotros, nosotras vemos = we see
ustedes ven = you see
ellos, ellas ven = they see

dar = to give
yo doy = I give
tú das = you give
usted da = you give
él, ella da = he, she, it gives
nosotros, nosotras damos = we give
ustedes dan = you give
ellos, ellas dan = they give

If you missed even one, the door
will not open for Enrique! So study until
you can fulfill the twisted door's demands!
When you have made no mistakes, you may go
on to Capítulo 39. A little word of warning:
Danger lurks behind one of the doors!

La puerta retorcida se abre por sí misma. . .
« Entremos, Francisca ».
Entramos por la puerta retorcida. Inmediatamente,
se cierra detrás de nosotros con el sonido de una puerta muy pesada.
« ¡Enrique, mira lo que hay frente a nosotros! ».
« ¡Vaya, otra puerta retorcida! ».
Pongo la mano sobre esta nueva puerta retorcida.
Inmediatamente después, letras doradas rodeadas por un tipo
de halo aparecen en la puerta creando las siguientes palabras:

HACER
HACE CALOR
HABER HECHO

The twisted door opens by itself . . .
« Let's enter, Francisca. »
We enter by way of the twisted door. Immediately,
it closes behind us with the sound of a very heavy door.
« Enrique, look at what there is in front of us! »
« Well, another twisted door! »
I place my hand on this new twisted door.
Immediately after, golden letters surrounded by a type
of halo appear on the door creating the following words:

TO DO
IT IS HOT (WEATHER)
TO HAVE DONE

Can you help Francisca with these words?
Her fate is in your hands!

First, conjugate the verb **hacer** for Francisca.
Then give the answers to the following:

1. it is hot (weather) = _____
2. it is cold = _____
3. it's windy = _____
4. I have done = _____
5. you (singular, polite) have done = _____
6. he has done = _____
7. we have done = _____
8. they have done = _____
9. you (plural) have done = _____
10. she has done = _____

Aquí están las respuestas:

hacer = to do; to make
yo hago = I do; I make
tú haces = you do; you make
usted hace = you do; you make
él, ella hace = he, she, it does; he, she, it makes
nosotros, nosotras hacemos = we do; we make
ustedes hacen = you do; you make
ellos, ellas hacen = they do; they make

1. hace calor
2. hace frío
3. hace viento
4. yo he hecho
5. usted ha hecho
6. él ha hecho
7. nosotros, nosotras hemos hecho
8. ellos, ellas han hecho
9. ustedes han hecho
10. ella ha hecho

If you missed even one, the door
will not open for Francisca! So study until
you can fulfill the twisted door's demands!
When you have made no mistakes, you may go
on to Capítulo 40. A little word of warning:
Danger lurks behind one of the doors!

La puerta retorcida se abre por sí misma. . .
« Entremos, Enrique ».
Entramos por la puerta retorcida. Inmediatamente,
se cierra detrás de nosotros con el sonido de una puerta muy pesada.
« ¡Francisca, mira lo que hay frente a nosotros! ».
« ¡Vaya, otra puerta retorcida! ».
Enrique pone su pequeña mano sobre esta nueva puerta retorcida.
Inmediatamente después, letras doradas rodeadas por un tipo
de halo aparecen en la puerta creando la siguiente palabra:

VOCABULARIO

The twisted door opens by itself . . .
« Let's enter, Enrique. »
We enter by way of the twisted door. Immediately,
it closes behind us with the sound of a very heavy door.
« Francisca, look at what there is in front of us! »
« Well, another twisted door! »
Enrique places his little hand on this new twisted door.
Immediately after, golden letters surrounded by a type
of halo appear on the door creating the following word:

VOCABULARY

Can you help Enrique with these words?
His fate is in your hands!

1. around = _____
2. por todos lados = _____
3. without = _____
4. to wait (for) = _____
5. the eyes = _____
6. like; as = _____
7. bien = _____
8. more = _____
9. casi = _____
10. the head = _____
11. adivinar = _____
12. far = _____
13. igual = _____
14. the stone = _____
15. entonces = _____
16. to forget = _____
17. encontrar = _____
18. the forehead = _____
19. ya = _____
20. despite = _____

Aquí están las respuestas:

1. alrededor
2. everywhere
3. sin
4. esperar
5. los ojos
6. como
7. well
8. más
9. almost; nearly
10. la cabeza
11. to guess
12. lejos
13. the same
14. la piedra
15. then
16. olvidar
17. to find
18. la frente
19. already
20. a pesar de

If you missed even one, the door
will not open for Enrique! So study until
you can fulfill the twisted door's demands!
When you have made no mistakes, you may go
on to Capítulo 41. A little word of warning:
Danger lurks behind one of the doors!

La puerta retorcida se abre por sí misma. . .
« Entremos, Francisca ».
Entramos por la puerta retorcida. Inmediatamente,
se cierra detrás de nosotros con el sonido de una puerta muy pesada.
« ¡Enrique, mira lo que hay frente a nosotros! ».
« ¡Vaya, otra puerta retorcida! ».
Pongo la mano sobre esta nueva puerta retorcida.
Inmediatamente después, letras doradas rodeadas por un tipo
de halo aparecen en la puerta creando la siguiente palabra:

DIVERSO

The twisted door opens by itself . . .
« Let's enter, Francisca. »
We enter by way of the twisted door. Immediately,
it closes behind us with the sound of a very heavy door.
« Enrique, look at what there is in front of us! »
« Well, another twisted door! »
I place my hand on this new twisted door.
Immediately after, golden letters surrounded by a type
of halo appear on the door creating the following word:

DIVERSE

Can you help Francisca with these words?
Her fate is in your hands!

1. I cannot = _____
2. it is a face = _____
3. where are we? = _____
4. la tristeza = _____
5. better = _____
6. close; near(by) = _____
7. we have to answer = _____
8. a light = _____
9. the pain = _____
10. a thunderstorm = _____
11. sobre = _____
12. una pista = _____
13. to touch = _____
14. alguien = _____
15. burlarse de = _____
16. with care; carefully = _____
17. the knee = _____
18. frente a = _____
19. the voice = _____
20. entre = _____

Aquí están las respuestas:

1. (yo) no puedo
2. es una cara
3. ¿dónde estamos?
4. the sadness
5. mejor
6. cerca
7. nosotros, nosotras tenemos que responder
8. una luz
9. el dolor
10. una tormenta
11. on; upon
12. a track; a clue
13. tocar
14. someone; somebody
15. to make fun of
16. con cuidado
17. la rodilla
18. in front of; opposite
19. la voz
20. between

If you missed even one, the door
will not open for Francisca! So study until
you can fulfill the twisted door's demands!
When you have made no mistakes, you may go
on to Capítulo 42. A little word of warning:
Danger lurks behind one of the doors!

La puerta retorcida se abre por sí misma. . .
« Entremos, Enrique ».
Entramos por la puerta retorcida. Inmediatamente,
se cierra detrás de nosotros con el sonido de una puerta muy pesada.
« ¡Francisca, mira lo que hay frente a nosotros! ».
« ¡Vaya, otra puerta retorcida! ».
Enrique pone su pequeña mano sobre esta nueva puerta retorcida.
Inmediatamente después, letras doradas rodeadas por un tipo
de halo aparecen en la puerta creando la siguiente palabra:

VOCABULARIO

The twisted door opens by itself . . .
« Let's enter, Enrique. »
We enter by way of the twisted door. Immediately,
it closes behind us with the sound of a very heavy door.
« Francisca, look at what there is in front of us! »
« Well, another twisted door! »
Enrique places his little hand on this new twisted door.
Immediately after, golden letters surrounded by a type
of halo appear on the door creating the following word:

VOCABULARY

Can you help Enrique with these words and expressions?
His fate is in your hands!

1. la vida = _____
2. el agua = _____
3. cada = _____
4. the rain = _____
5. a smile = _____
6. the time; the weather = _____
7. a lot of = _____
8. por lo tanto = _____
9. why = _____
10. it is true = _____
11. again = _____
12. thank you = _____
13. now = _____
14. juntos = _____
15. who? = _____
16. good morning = _____
17. there is; there are = _____
18. on the contrary = _____
19. de acuerdo = _____
20. thus; in this way = _____

Aquí están las respuestas:

1. the life
2. the water
3. each
4. la lluvia
5. una sonrisa
6. el tiempo
7. mucho
8. therefore
9. por qué
10. es verdad
11. otra vez; nuevamente
12. gracias
13. ahora
14. together
15. ¿quién?
16. buenos días
17. hay
18. al contrario
19. all right; O.K.; agreed
20. así

If you missed even one, the door
will not open for Enrique! So study until
you can fulfill the twisted door's demands!
When you have made no mistakes, you may go
on to Capítulo 43. A little word of warning:
Danger lurks behind one of the doors!

La puerta retorcida se abre por sí misma. . .
« Entremos, Francisca ».
Entramos por la puerta retorcida. Inmediatamente,
se cierra detrás de nosotros con el sonido de una puerta muy pesada.
« ¡Enrique, mira lo que hay frente a nosotros! ».
« ¡Vaya, otra puerta retorcida! ».
Pongo la mano sobre esta nueva puerta retorcida.
Inmediatamente después, letras doradas rodeadas por un tipo
de halo aparecen en la puerta creando la siguiente palabra:

DIVERSO

The twisted door opens by itself . . .
« Let's enter, Francisca. »
We enter by way of the twisted door. Immediately,
it closes behind us with the sound of a very heavy door.
« Enrique, look at what there is in front of us! »
« Well, another twisted door! »
I place my hand on this new twisted door.
Immediately after, golden letters surrounded by a type
of halo appear on the door creating the following word:

DIVERSE

Can you help Francisca with these words?
Her fate is in your hands!

1. en efecto = _____
2. abrir = _____
3. algo = _____
4. esto es = _____
5. this is not = _____
6. in = _____
7. inside = _____
8. después = _____
9. suddenly = _____
10. I am a boy = _____
11. me neither = _____
12. tratar de recordar = _____
13. ¿podemos nosotros? = _____
14. malvado = _____
15. los dos = _____
16. allí = _____
17. ¿qué es esto? = _____
18. to cry = _____
19. creer = _____
20. to walk = _____

Aquí están las respuestas:

1. indeed
2. to open
3. something
4. this is
5. esto no es
6. en
7. dentro (de)
8. after; afterwards
9. de pronto; súbitamente; de repente
10. (yo) soy un niño
11. yo tampoco
12. to try to remember
13. can we?
14. evil; wicked
15. both
16. there
17. what is this?
18. llorar
19. to believe
20. caminar

If you missed even one, the door
will not open for Francisca! So study until
you can fulfill the twisted door's demands!
When you have made no mistakes, you may go
on to Capítulo 44. A little word of warning:
Danger lurks behind one of the doors!

NOTAS

CAPÍTULO CUARENTA Y CUATRO 44

« Francisca, estoy cansado. Hemos pasado
por al menos ocho puertas retorcidas.
¿Alguna vez se va a terminar esto? ».
« Enrique, tienes que ser valiente. No olvides que la pintura bonita
nos dijo que pasáramos a través de las puertas retorcidas.
No tenemos elección. Debemos tratar
de hacer lo que ella nos dijo ».
Él suspira. . .

Otra vez, Enrique avanza hacia una puerta retorcida.
Tan pronto como llega al umbral de la puerta, vemos
que ésta no es como las otras:
¡una cara sobrenatural con rasgos iluminados aparece súbitamente
sobre la puerta retorcida! Los pequeños ojos negros
penetran hasta lo más profundo de nuestras almas.
La enorme boca, que enmarca un infinito espacio negro,
articula las siguientes palabras:

**« Ustedes nunca van a salir de aquí, niños.
¡Ustedes son míos! »,**

declara el espectro con una voz tan tronante que las
vibraciones sacuden el pasillo.

145

Enrique está aterrorizado frente a la puerta retorcida.
El fantasma se aprovecha de esto:
una gran mano con un largo brazo que parece surgir
de la superficie de la puerta agarra al pobre Enrique. . .
La mano fantasmagórica sujeta el cuerpo del pequeño Enrique
con un terrible apretón y **lo aleja de la puerta**.
« ¡Francisca! ¡Ayúdame! ».
Corro hacia Enrique para ayudarlo. Cuando llego hasta él, una cosa nefasta
sucede: pierdo el equilibrio y me caigo al piso.
Absolutamente desesperada, extiendo la mano hacia Enrique,
quien está tratando de liberarse dando patadas.
Estos movimientos distraen a la aparición por un momento.
Logro pasar la mano entre los pies de Enrique
y así **toco** la parte inferior de la puerta retorcida.
El fantasma deja escapar un grito que parece venir del infierno.
¡Pero él sujeta a Enrique aún más fuerte!
Súbitamente, letras doradas rodeadas por un tipo
de halo se sobreponen en la horrible frente del fantasma
creando la siguiente palabra:

SALIR

« ¡Dios mío! ¡Estoy demasiado asustada para recordar
cómo conjugar **SALIR**! ¡Socorro! ».

« Francisca, I'm tired. We have gone through
at least eight twisted doors.
Is this ever going to end? »
« Enrique, you have to be brave. Don't forget that the pretty painting
told us to go through the twisted doors.
We don't have a choice. We must try
to do what it told us. »
He sighs . . .

Once again, Enrique moves on toward a twisted door.
As soon as he arrives at the door's threshold, we see
that this one is not like the others:
A supernatural face with illuminated features suddenly appears
on the twisted door! The little black eyes
penetrate to the very depths of our souls.
The enormous mouth, framing a black infinite space,
articulates the following words:

« You are never going to get out of here, children.
You are mine! »

declares the specter with such a thunderous voice that the
vibrations shake the hall.
Enrique is terror-stricken in front of the twisted door.
The phantom takes advantage of this:
A large hand with a long arm seeming to arise
from the surface of the door grabs poor Enrique . . .
The ghostly hand holds little Enrique's body
with a terrible grip and **moves him away from the door**.
« Francisca! Help me! »
I run toward Enrique to help him. When I reach him, an ill-fated thing
happens: I lose my balance and fall to the ground.
In sheer desperation, I extend my hand toward Enrique
who is trying to kick himself free.
These movements distract the apparition for a moment.
I manage to pass my hand between Enrique's feet
and thereby **touch** the bottom part of the twisted door.
The phantom lets out a cry that seems to come from hell.
But he holds Enrique even tighter!
Suddenly, golden letters surrounded by a type
of halo superimpose themselves on the hideous forehead of the phantom
creating the following words:

TO GO OUT

« My goodness! I'm too afraid to remember
how to conjugate **TO GO OUT**! *Help! »*

Can you help conjugate **SALIR** for Francisca?
If not, Francisca and Enrique will be prisoners in this
terrible house forever!

Aquí están las respuestas:

salir = to go out; to leave
yo salgo = I go out
tú sales = you go out
usted sale = you go out
él, ella, sale = he, she, it goes out
nosotros, nosotras salimos = we go out
ustedes salen = you go out
ellos, ellas salen = they go out

If you missed even one, Francisca and Enrique are doomed!
You must study and get it right for their sake!
When you have made no mistakes,
you may go on to Capítulo 45 . . .
if you dare!

NOTAS

Me levanto rápidamente. ¡Gracias a la ayuda de un
buen samaritano, recuerdo la conjugación
del verbo **SALIR**!

Recito:

salir = to go out
yo salgo
tú sales
usted sale
él, ella sale
nosotros, nosotras salimos
ustedes salen
ellos, ellas salen

Inmediatamente oigo un alarido abominable:
« **¡Ahhhhh!** ».
La enorme boca del fantasma se ensancha aún más
para revelar un espacio negro, infinito y macabro.
¡Es obvio que la intención del espectro es tragarnos!
Ahora, la puerta retorcida se abre. . .

I get up quickly. Thanks to the help of a
good Samaritan, I remember the conjugation
*of the verb, **TO GO OUT**!*

I recite:

to go out = salir
I go out
you go out
you go out
he, she goes out
we go out
you go out
they go out

I immediately hear an abominable howl,
*« **Ahhhhh!** »*
The enormous mouth of the phantom widens even more
to reveal a black, infinite, macabre space.
It is obvious that the specter's intention is to swallow us!
Now, the twisted door opens . . .

NOTAS

Todo huele bien. . . Aire fresco. Luz. . .
Luz natural. . .
Estoy afuera. ¡Salí de la casa!
¡Qué vergüenza!
Por algunos segundos, me olvidé de mi pobre Enrique.
¡Qué final tan atroz!
No hay duda de que se lo tragó el fantasma. . .
Empiezo a llorar.
« Mi pobre Enrique. Estoy tan triste.
¡Te extraño! ».
« ¡Yo también te extraño! ».
¡Levanto la mirada y veo frente a mí, al pequeño
Enrique sano y salvo!
Nos abrazamos fuertemente.
« Francisca, ahora tengo una pequeña sorpresa para ti ».
Me doy la vuelta.
« ¡Gracias, Francisca! », dicen **ellos**.
« Francisca, tengo el gran honor de presentarte a
mis padres, el señor y la señora Woodward ».
« Francisca, tú nos has salvado a todos ».
« Encantada de conocerlos, pero me temo que no entiendo ».
« Ahora entenderás », dice el Sr. Woodward.
« Sin embargo, yo te ayudé un poquito también », dice riendo.
Estoy totalmente confundida.
« ¿Recuerdas el viento? ».

« Sí, por supuesto. Gracias al viento logramos
salir del cementerio ».
El Sr. Woodward exclama:
« ¡Yo era el viento! ».
« Y yo era la 'pintura bonita', como tú dices »,
afirma la Sra. Woodward.
La Sra. Woodward continúa su explicación:
« Todos nosotros fuimos tomados como cautivos en la casa
por el malvado fantasma. El espectro
nos transformó para que no pudiésemos
ayudar a Enrique. Entre otras cosas, el fantasma borró de
su memoria todo acerca de nuestra existencia ».
La interrumpo:
« Me parecía raro que él nunca hablara de sus padres ».
« Sí », continúa la Sra. Woodward,
« así Enrique no podía buscarnos ».
« Sin duda el fantasma pensó que íbamos a estar
cautivos por toda la eternidad. ¡Él nunca podría haberse imaginado
que una niña como tú vendría y nos salvaría!
¡Ése fue su mayor error!
Si se hubiese dado cuenta, te habría transformado a ti también ».
« ¡Y nosotros estaríamos todavía en esa casa! », digo temblando.
La Sra. Woodward me toma en sus brazos.
« No te preocupes, Francisca, tú estás sana y salva ».
Recobrando el ánimo, digo:
« Sr. Woodward, Sra. Woodward y mi pequeño Enrique,
ahora yo debo ir a casa. . . Mis padres deben de
estar muy preocupados. ¡Ellos no van a creerme
cuando les explique que estuve en una casa embrujada! ».
« **¡Peor para ti!** ».
« ¿Quién dijo eso? ».
« ¡Yo no! ».
« ¡Yo tampoco! ».
« ¡Ni yo! ».
« ¡Ohhhh, no vamos a empezar esto otra vez! ».

Everything smells good . . . Fresh air. Light . . .
Natural light . . .
I am outside. I got out of the house!
How shameful!
For a few seconds, I forgot about my poor Enrique.
What an atrocious end!
There is no doubt that he was swallowed up by the phantom . . .
I start to cry.
« My poor Enrique. I am so sad.
I miss you! »
« I miss you too! »
I raise my eyes and see in front of me little
Enrique safe and sound!
We hug each other tightly.
« Francisca, now I have a little surprise for you. »
I turn around.
« Thank you, Francisca! » **they** *say.*
« Francisca, I have the great honor of presenting to you
my parents, Mr. and Mrs. Woodward. »
« Francisca, you have saved us all. »
« Pleased to meet you, but I fear that I do not understand. »
« Now you will (understand), » says Mr. Woodward.
« However, I helped you a little bit also, » he says laughing.
I am totally confused.
« Do you remember the wind? »
« Yes, of course. Thanks to the wind, we succeeded in
getting out of the cemetery. »
Mr. Woodward exclaims,
« It was I, the wind! »
« And it was I the 'pretty painting,' as you say, »
asserts Mrs. Woodward.
Mrs. Woodward continues her explanation:
« We were all taken as captives in the house
by the wicked phantom. The specter
transformed us so that we could not
help Enrique. Among other things, the phantom erased from
his memory everything concerning our existence. »
I interrupt her:
« I found it odd that he never spoke of his parents. »
« Yes, » continues Mrs. Woodward,
« this way Enrique couldn't look for us. »
« The phantom surely thought that we were to be
captives for eternity. He could never have imagined
that a little girl like you would come and save us!
That was his biggest mistake!
If he had realized, he would have transformed you too. »
« And we would still be in that house! » I say trembling.

Mrs. Woodward takes me in her arms.
« Don't worry, Francisca, you are safe and sound. »
Regaining my courage, I say,
·« Mr. Woodward, Mrs. Woodward, and my little Enrique,
now I must go home . . . My parents must
be very worried. They are never going to believe me
when I explain to them that I was in a haunted house! »
*« **Too bad for you!** »*
« Who said that? »
« Not me! »
« Me neither! »
« Nor I! »
« Ohhhh, we're not going to start this all over again! »

~~ GLOSARIO ~~

Key: *m* = masculine; *f* = feminine; *s* = singular; *pl* = plural; *adj* = adjective;
( ) = contents precede the entry in the story; numeral = chapter number

a = at; to, 3
abrazar = to hug, 46
abrir = to open, 5
acá = here, 32
acabar de = to have just, 23
acerca de = about; concerning, 46
acercarse a = to approach, 17
actuar = to act, 25
además = besides; moreover; what's
    more, 10
adiós = farewell; goodbye, 29
adivinanza *f* = riddle, 33
adivinar = to guess, 33
adónde = where, 19
afortunadamente = fortunately;
    luckily, 25
afuera = outside, 18
agarrar = to grab, 44
agua *f* = water, 26
agujero *m* = hole, 12
ahí = there, 24
ahora = now, 30
aire *m* = air; look, 4
al = to the, 7
alarido *m* = howl; shriek, 45
alboroto *m* = racket; din, 30
al contrario = on the contrary, 32
alegría *f* = joy; happiness, 30
alejar = to move away, 44
algo = something, 10
alguien = someone; somebody, 24
algún *m adj* = some; any, 31
alguna *f adj* = any, 26
alguna vez = ever, 26
algunos = a few, 46
aliento *m* = breath, 23
allí = there; over there, 12
alma *f* = soul, 44
al menos = at least, 44

al mismo tiempo = at the same time;
    together, 17
al principio = at first, 28
alrededor = around, 19
alta *f adj* = tall; high; loud, 9
amarillo *m adj* = yellow, 14
anaranjado *m adj* = orange, 14
ánimo *m* = spirit; courage; heart, 21
apagarse = to go out; to switch off, 33
apenas = barely; hardly, 24
a pesar de = despite, 18
apresurarse = to hurry, 33
apretón *m* = grip; squeeze, 44
aprovecharse de = to take advantage
    of, 29
apuro (me) = I hurry, 23
aquí = here, 22
armarse de = to summon up, 22
arrodillarse = to kneel (down), 25
arrojar = to throw; to hurl, 18
arrojarse = to throw oneself, 18
así = thus; in this way; thereby; so, 32
asombrosa *f adj* = amazing;
    astonishing, 23
asustada *f adj* = afraid; scared, 10
a su vez = in turn, 25
atacar = to attack, 23
aterrorizado *m adj* = terror-stricken;
    terrified, 44
atraer = to attract, 19
atrás = backwards; behind, 21
a través de = across; through, 44
atreverse = to dare, 32
atroz *m,f adj* = atrocious, 46
aumentar = to increase, 27
aun = even, 35
aún = still, 11
aunque = even if, 33
avanzar = to move forward, 10

a veces = sometimes, 32
avergonzar = to embarrass, 22
averiguar = to find out, 12
¡ay! = ouch!, 11
ayudar = to help, 22
azul *m,f adj* = blue, 14

bajar = to lower, 20
bajo = under, 22
bastante = quite, 19
batalla *f* = battle, 27
bien = well, 13, 34
blanco *m adj* = white, 14
bloquear = to block (off), 16
boca *f* = mouth, 20
bonita *f adj* = pretty, 32
borde *m* = edge, 35
borrar = to erase, 46
borroso *m adj* = blurred; blurry;
    hazy, 28
brazo *m* = arm, 20
bruscamente = abruptly, 23
bueno = good; all right, 31
buenos días = good morning, 31
burlarse de = to make fun of;
    to mock, 25
buscar = to look for, 46

cabeza *f* = head, 20
cada *m,f adj* = each, 24
cada vez más = more and more, 24
cadena *f* = chain, 29
caer = to fall, 10
caigo = I fall (See *caer*), 44
cállate = be quiet, 19
cambiar = to change, 30
caminar = to walk, 18
caminar hacia = to walk towards, 18
camuflar = to camouflage;
    to disguise, 23
cansado *m adj* = tired, 44
cara *f* = face, 15
¡caramba! = good gracious!, 12
casi = almost, 21
cautivo *m* = captive, 46

cayendo = falling (See *caer*), 12
cerca = close; near(by), 23
cerca (de) = closely; close up, 24
cerrar = to close, 7
chirrido *m* = squeaking; creaking, 31
chupete *m* = pacifier; lollipop, 11
cielo *m* = sky; heaven, 18
cierra = he closes (See *cerrar*), 26
cierto *m adj* = certain, 26
cinco = five, 3
colgar = to hang, 13
colocar = to place; to put, 23
comenzar = to begin, 9
comienzo = I begin (See *comenzar*), 9
como = like; as; since, 27
cómo = how, 15
¿cómo es que? = how is it that?;
    how come . . .?, 15
¿cómo estás tú? = how are you?, 34
comprender = to understand, 25
con = with, 5
con calma = calmly, 20
con cuidado = carefully; with care, 24
confundir = to confuse, 46
conmoción *f* = shock, 30
conmover = to overcome with
    emotion; to move, 22
conocer = to know; to meet, 46
consentido *m adj* = spoiled, 19
contar = to tell; to count, 5
contestar = to reply; to answer, 20
corazón *m* = heart, 10
corremos = we run (See *correr*), 11
correr = to run; to flow, 11
corro = I run (See *correr*), 9
cortar = to cut, 23
cortarme el aliento = to knock the
    breath out of me; to take my
    breath away, 23
cosa *f* = thing, 14
creer = to believe; to think, 10
creo = I believe (See *creer*), 32
crujido *m* = creaking, 31
cruzar = to cross, 21
cuando = when, 28
cuatro = four, 3
cubrir = to cover; to protect, 21

cuenta de (darse) = to realize, 22
cuéntame = tell me (See *contar*), 20
cuerpo *m* = body, 18
cuidado *m* = care, 10
cuidado (con) = carefully; with care, 24

dame = give me, 29
dando = giving (See *dar*), 44
dar = to give, 29
darle = to give him; her; it; you
　　(*s, polite*), 27
darse cuenta de = to realize, 24
darse la vuelta = to turn around, 33
de = of; from; made of, 10
de acuerdo = all right; O.K.;
　　agreed, 32
deber = must, 26
débil = feeble; weak, 32
decepción *f* = disappointment, 30
decimos = we say (See *decir*), 17
decir = to say; to tell, 31
dedo *m* = finger, 4
de inmediato = immediately, 19
dejar = to leave, 44
déjeme = let me, 8
del = of the, 7
deletrear = to spell (out), 24
demasiado = too; too much, 11
dentro de = inside, 15
de pronto = suddenly, 11
de repente = suddenly, 16
descansar = to rest, 22
desde = from; since, 33
deslumbrante *adj* = dazzling, 23
después = after; afterwards; then, 22
después de todo = after all, 22
destino *m* = destiny, 23
detener = to stop, 18
detrás de = behind, 7
día *m* = day, 31
dice = he says (See *decir*), 5
diez = ten, 3
dime = tell me, 30
doler = to hurt, 11
dolor *m* = pain, 23
¿dónde estamos? = where are we?, 13

dos = two, 3
duda *f* = doubt, 12
dulce *m,f adj* = sweet, 32

e = and (Before *i* or *hi*), 23
echar un vistazo = to cast a glance;
　　to have a quick look at, 33
efectivamente = indeed, 9
el *m* = the, 7
él *m* = he; it, 1
elección *f* = choice, 44
ella *f* = she; it, 1
ellas *f* = they, 1
ellos *m* = they, 1
embrujada *f adj* = haunted, 46
empapado hasta los huesos (estar) =
　　to be soaked to the skin (bone), 26
empapar = to soak; to drench, 26
empezar = to begin, 8
empujar = to push; to shove, 12
en = in; on, 6
encontrar = to find, 24
en efecto = indeed, 14
enemigo *m* = enemy, 33
enfocarse = to focus, 34
enfrentar = to face; to confront, 33
engañar = to deceive; to fool, 29
enmarcar = to frame, 44
ennegrecer = to blacken, 33
enojarse = to get mad, 31
en realidad = in fact, 1
ensanchar = to widen, 45
entender = to understand, 33
entiendo = I understand (See
　　entender), 25
entonces = then; so; at that time, 21
entrar = to enter, 35
entre = between, 26
en voz alta = aloud; out loud; in a
　　loud voice, 9
eres = you (*s, familiar*) are (See *ser*), 1
erguirse = to straighten up, 22
error *m* = mistake, 46
es = you (*s, polite*) are; he, she, it is
　　(See *ser*), 1
esas *f, pl adj* = those, 15

escapar = to escape, 16
escombros *m* = debris, 24
esconder = to hide, 22
escribir = to write, 12
escrito *m adj* = written, 12
escuchado = listened; heard, 32
escuchar = to listen; to hear, 26
escucho = I listen; I hear
 (See *escuchar*), 22
es decir = that is to say, 17
es falso = it is false, 28
esforzarse = to make an effort, 22
esfuerzo *m* = effort, 27
eslabón *m* = link, 29
eso *neutral* = that, 15
eso me duele = that hurts (See *doler*), 11
eso significa = that means, 17
espacio *m* = space, 44
espantoso *m adj* = dreadful; appalling;
 frightening, 29
especialmente = especially, 21
espeluznante *adj* = hair-raising;
 horrifying, 21
esperanza *f* = hope, 16
esperar = to wait (for); to expect, 19
espesar = to thicken, 28
espíritu *m* = spirit, 22
esta *f adj* = this, 15
ésta *f* = this one, 15
está = you (*s, polite*) are; he, she, it is
 (See *estar*), 2
estamos = we are (See *estar*), 2
están = you (*pl*) are; they are
 (See *estar*), 2
estar = to be, 2
estar en juego = to be at stake, 25
estar equivocada = to be wrong, 25
estar vivo = to be alive, 34
éstas *f, pl* = these (ones), 15
estás = you (*s, familiar*) are
 (See *estar*), 2
estás contando = you are counting, 5
este *m adj* = this, 15
esto *neutral* = this, 15
esto significa = this means, 17
estoy = I am (See *estar*), 2
estrechas *f, pl adj* = narrow, 26

estruendo *m* = crash (of thunder), 24
estudiar = to study, 30
es verdad = it is true, 28
exigir = to demand, 12
explicar = to explain, 46
extender = to hold out; to stretch out, 21
exterior *m* = exterior; outside, 18
extraña *f adj* = strange; bizarre, 13
extrañar = to miss, 46
extraño *m adj* = strange; bizarre, 14
extraño (te) = I miss you
 (See *extrañar*), 46

falso *m adj* = false, 28
fantasma *m* = ghost; phantom, 8
fea *f adj* = ugly, 6
feo *m adj* = ugly, 6
fijamente = fixedly, 20
fina *f adj* = thin; fine, 24
final *m* = end, 46
forma *f* = shape; way, 28
formada *f adj* = fashioned; shaped;
 formed, 23
formar = to form; to make, 23
fortuna *f* = fortune; luck, 25
frente *f* = forehead, 22
frente a = opposite; in front of, 25
fresco = fresh, 46
frío = cold, 25
fuente *f* = source, 33
fuerte = hard; loud(ly); strong, 7
fuertemente = strongly; tightly, 46
fuerza *f* = force; strength; might, 21

girar = to turn; to spin, 23
golpeo = I hit; I pound (on); I bang
 (on), 9
gota *f* = drop, 22
grabar = to engrave, 22
gracias = thank you, 29
grado *m* = degree, 26
grande *m,f adj* = big; large, 1
grave *m,f adj* = serious; low, 29
gris *m,f adj* = gray, 18
grisáceo *m adj* = grayish, 28

gritar = to shout; to scream; to cry (out); to yell, 17

grito *m* = cry; shout, 18

grito con todas mis fuerzas = I shout with all my might; I yell at the top of my voice, 30

gruñido *m* = growl, 29

haber = to have (Helping verb), 31

habitación *f* = room, 31

hablar = to speak; to talk, 32

hace calor = it's hot (weather), 25

hace frío = it's cold (weather), 25

hacer = to do; to make, 19

hace viento = it's windy, 25

hacia = toward(s); in the direction of, 9

hacia atrás = backwards, 21

haciendo = doing; making, 24

ha hablado = he, she, it has spoken; you (*s, polite*) have spoken (See *hablar*), 32

halar = to pull, 7

halo *m* = halo (Not commonly used in spoken Spanish), 35

hasta = (right) to; as far as; up to; even, 26

hay = there is; there are (See *haber*), 21

hombre *m* = man, 3

hombro *m* = shoulder, 20

hondo *m adj* = deep, 26

horrible *m,f adj* = horrible; hideous, 44

huele = he, she, it smells; you smell (*s, polite*) (See *oler*), 46

hueso *m* = bone, 26

igual *m,f adj* = the same; equal, 23

inclinada *f adj* = slanted, 23

inclinarse = to lean over, 23

increíble *adj* = incredible; unbelievable, 30

inferior *m,f adj* = lower, 26

inmediatamente = immediately, 30

interrumpir = to interrupt; to cut short, 19

ir = to go, 26

jalar = to pull, 7

juego *m* = game, 25

juntos = together, 16

la *f* = the; it, 7

labio *m* = lip, 20

lado *m* = side, 19

lágrima *f* = tear, 15

lápida *f* = tombstone, 19

largo *m adj* = long, 44

las *f, pl* = the; them; you; those, 7

lastimarse = to hurt oneself, 13

latir = to beat, 10

le = him; her; you (*s, polite*), 27

leer = to read, 24

lejos = far, 34

lentamente = slowly, 5

les = you (*pl*); them, 27

letra *f* = letter, 24

levantar = to raise (up), 46

levantarse = to get up, 28

limpieza *f* = cleaning, 21

linda *f adj* = cute, 15

línea *f* = line, 26

llamarse = to be named; to call oneself, 6

llegar = to arrive, 44

llegar hasta = to reach (up to), 44

llego = I arrive (See *llegar*), 3

llenar = to fill, 15

llorar = to cry; to weep, 10

lloriquear = to snivel; to whimper; to whine, 22

lluvia *f* = rain, 27

lo = him; it, 20

lodo *m* = mud, 27

lograr = to achieve; to succeed, 30

¡lo logré! = I did it!; I succeeded!, 10

lo que = what, 10

los *m, pl* = the; them; you; those, 7

los dos = both, 16

luces *f, pl* = lights, 33

luego = then; later (on); afterwards; next, 20

lugar *m* = place, 22

luz *f* = light, 23

madera *f* = wood, 6
mal = bad(ly); poorly, 34
maligna *f adj* = evil, 32
malvado *m adj* = evil; wicked, 16
manera *f* = way; manner, 23
mano *f* = hand, 20
marco *m* = frame, 35
marear = to make dizzy, 23
marrón *m,f adj* = brown, 18
más = more, 20
más (cada vez) = more and more, 24
más lejos = farther, 34
matar = to kill, 21
mayor (su) = his biggest, 46
me = myself; me, 6, 27
mejilla *f* = cheek, 20
mejor *m,f adj* = better, 32
menos (al) = at least, 44
mi *m,f adj* = my, 7
mí = me, 7
miedo *m* = fear, 2
mientras = while; as, 11
minúscula *f adj* = minuscule; tiny, 24
mío *m* = mine, 44
mirada *f* = look; gaze, 3
mira fijamente (me) = he fixes his gaze
    upon me; he stares at me, 20
mirar = to look (at), 13
miro = I look (at) (See *mirar*), 3
misma (por sí) = by itself, 36
mismo = same, 17
mojar = to wet; to moisten, 27
morado *m adj* = purple, 18
morder = to bite, 26
morir = to die, 24
moverse = to move, 7
movimiento *m* = movement; motion, 23
muchas *f, pl adj* = many; a lot of, 6
mucho = a lot of; a lot; much; very
    (much), 2, 17
mucho más = much more, 20
mucho tiempo = a lot of time, 17
muerte *f* = death, 26
mundo *m* = world, 22
muy = very, 27

nada = nothing, 30
nadie = nobody, 33
naranja = orange, 18
nariz *f* = nose, 20
negro *m adj* = black, 14
negruzco *m adj* = blackish, 33
ningún *m adj* = any; no, 31
niña *f* = child; (little) girl, 12
niño *m* = child; (little) boy, 12
niños *m, pl* = children, 12
ni siquiera = not even, 23
no = no; not; never, 8
¿no es así? = isn't that so?, 34
no hay = there is not; there are not, 32
no. . . más = not . . . any more, 30
nombre *m* = name, 22
no me gusta = I don't like (it), 19
no me hagas = don't make me, 19
no. . . nada = nothing, 30
no. . . nada más = not . . . anything
    else, 30
no. . . ni. . . ni = neither . . . nor, 22
no. . . nunca = never, 30
no puedo = I cannot (See *poder*), 8
nos = ourselves; us, 6, 27
no son = they are not (See *ser*), 14
nosotras *f* = we, 1
nosotros *m* = we, 1
no soy = I am not (See *ser*), 8
notar = to notice, 30
no tener razón = to be wrong, 25
no veo = I do not see (See *ver*), 17
no veo nada = I do not see anything, 17
nube *f* = cloud, 18
nuestro = our; (of) ours, 19
nuevamente = again, 20
nueve = nine, 3
nunca = never; ever, 32

o = or, 18
ocho = eight, 3
oído *m* = ear, 18
oigo = I hear (See *oír*), 10
oímos = we hear (See *oír*), 12
oír = to hear, 10
ojos *m, pl* = eyes, 20

óleo *m* = oil (painting), 30
oler = to smell, 46
olvidar = to forget, 23
opción *f* = choice, 32
oreja *f* = ear, 20
orgullosa *f adj* = proud, 23
oscura *f adj* = dark, 10
otra *f* = another (one); other (one), 29
otra vez = again; once again, 29
otro *m adj* = another, 17

padres *m, pl* = parents, 46
palabra *f* = word, 21
paleta *f* = lollipop, 11
palidecer = to turn pale, 15
para = for; to; in order to, 16
parar = to stop, 31
pararse = to stand (up), 28
para siempre = forever, 7
parecer = to look; to look like;
   to seem, 25
pared *f* = wall, 13
parlante *m,f adj* = talking, 32
pasar por = to go through, 32
pasar por alto = to miss; to pass over, 24
pasillo *m* = hall(way); corridor, 11
paso *m* = step, 18
patada *f* = kick, 44
pegado *m adj* = stuck; glued, 11
peligro *m* = danger, 33
pelo *m* = hair, 20
pensar = to think, 16
peor = worse, 26
¡peor para él! = too bad for him!, 19
pequeño = little; little one, 10
perder = to lose; to miss, 21
perdido *m adj* = lost, 27
permanecer = to stay, 32
pero = but, 9
perseguir = to pursue; to chase, 11
pesada *f adj* = heavy, 35
pesar *m* = sorrow; regret, 22
pie *m* = foot, 24
piedra *f* = stone, 21
pienso = I think (See *pensar*), 16
pierdo = I lose (See *perder*), 44

pierna *f* = leg, 20
pintar = to paint, 24
pintura *f* = painting, 13
pintura al óleo = oil painting, 30
piruleta *f* = lollipop, 11
pirulí *m* = lollipop, 11
piso *m* = floor; ground, 30
pista *f* = track; clue, 29
pobre *m,f adj* = poor, 17
poco = little; not much, 22
poco a poco = little by little;
   progressively, 17
podemos = we can (See *poder*), 16
poder = to be able to; can, 25
polvo *m* = dust, 21
poner = to place; to put, 35
ponerse = to become, 21
ponerse de pie = to stand up, 24
poquito (un) = a little bit, 46
por = for; because of; along; by, 13
por eso = that's why, 29
por lo tanto = therefore, 28
porque = because, 17
por qué = why, 23
por sí misma *f* = by itself, 17
por supuesto = of course, 46
por todos lados = everywhere, 19
pregunta *f* = question, 20
preguntar = to ask, 32
preocupado *m adj* = worried, 19
preocuparse = to worry, 22
presenciar = to witness, 33
presionar = to press (down) (on), 23
prestamos atención = we pay
   attention, 22
prestar atención = to pay attention, 22
profundo *m adj* = deep, 44
proteger = to protect, 25
prueba *f* = proof, 22
puedo = I can (See *poder*), 8
puerta *f* = door, 3
¡pum! = thud!; bang!, 30
punta *f* = tip, 23

que = that; which; who, 10
qué = what; how, 12

quedarse = to stay, 6
¿qué es eso? = what is that?, 17
¿qué es esto? = what is this?, 10
querer = to want, 19
querer decir = to mean, 32
¿quién? = who?, 19
¿quieres? = do you want? (See *querer*), 5
quiero = I want (See *querer*), 19
quizás = perhaps, 32

ráfaga *f* = gust, 23
rápidamente = fast; quickly, 29
rápido = quickly; quick; fast, 16
raro *m adj* = odd, 46
rasgos *m, pl* = features, 44
rayo *m* = lightning; streak or flash of
    lightning, 26
reconocer = to recognize, 28
recordar = to remember; to remind; to
    bring to mind, 25
reflexionar = to think; to think over; to
    reflect (on), 17
regresar = to go back, 19
reír = to laugh, 8
relámpago *m* = flash of lightning, 24
remolino *m* = whirlwind, 24
resbalar = to slip, 28
resonante *m,f adj* = resonant, 29
respirar = to breathe, 34
respirar hondo = to take a deep
    breath; to breathe deeply, 26
responder = to answer, 22
respuesta *f* = answer; reply, 20
resuelta *f adj* = resolute; determined, 32
retorcida *f adj* = twisted, 14
riendo = laughing (See *reír*), 46
risa *m* = laugh, 29
rodear = to surround, 35
rodilla *f* = knee, 25
rojo *m adj* = red, 14
rosa = pink, 18
rosado *m adj* = pink, 18
rugido *m* = roar; howl, 27
ruido *m* = noise, 31

saber = to know, 16
sabes = you (*s, familiar*) know
    (See *saber*), 16
sacudir = to shake, 44
salida *f* = exit, 16
salir = to go out; to leave; to get out, 24
saltar = to jump, 30
salvar = to save, 23
salvo *m adj* = safe, 46
sano *m adj* = healthy; sound, 46
sano y salvo = safe and sound
    (Literal: sound and safe), 46
se = himself; herself; yourself;
    yourselves; themselves; itself;
    oneself, 6
sé = I know (See *saber*), 12
secar = to dry; to wipe, 27
seguir = to follow, 24
segundo *m* = second, 46
seguro *m adj* = sure; certain, 15
seis = six, 3
semana *f* = week, 10
sentir = to feel, 25
señalar = to point, 34
ser = to be, 1
ser *m* = being, 28
se yergue = he straightens up
    (See *erguirse*), 22
si = if, 12
sí = yes, 20
sí = itself, 36
siempre = always, 30
siempre. . . todo = always . . .
    everything, 30
siete = seven, 3
significado *m* = meaning; significance, 31
significar = to mean, 9
siguiente *m,f adj* = following
    (See *seguir*), 19
silbar = to whistle, 18
sí misma (por) = by itself, 36
simular = to feign, 27
sin = without, 21
sin duda = surely; without doubt, 12
sin embargo = however; nevertheless;
    yet, 17
sino = but, 33

siquiera (ni) = not even, 23
sobre = on (top of); upon, 22
sobrenatural *adj* = supernatural;
    unearthly, 28
sobresaltarse = to jump; to start, 32
¡socorro! = help!, 44
sola *f adj* = alone; by itself, 8
solamente = only, 8
soldado *m* = soldier, 22
solo *m adj* = on one's own; by oneself, 26
sombra *f* = shadow, 33
somos = we are (See *ser*), 1
son = you (*pl*) are; they are (See *ser*), 1
sonido *m* = sound, 29
sonreír = to smile, 22
sonrisa *f* = smile, 27
soplar = to blow, 18
sorpresa *f* = surprise, 46
soy = I am (See *ser*), 1
su/sus = his; her; your; their; its;
    one's, 15
suave *m,f adj* = soft; smooth; gentle, 34
súbitamente = suddenly, 27
suceder = to happen, 23
sudor *m* = sweat, 22
suelo *m* = ground; floor, 28
sujetar = to hold (down), 44
sujeto *m* = subject, 29
suplicar = to beg, 22
surgir = to arise; to emerge, 28
suspirar = to sigh, 32
susurrar = to whisper, 20
suyo = his, 23

tamaño *m* = size, 19
también = too; also, 13
tampoco = neither, 17
tan = so; such, 10
tan pronto como = as soon as, 28
taparse = to cover oneself, 18
tarde = late, 11
te = yourself; you (*s, familiar*), 6, 27
temblar = to tremble; to shiver;
    to shake, 8
temer = to fear, 30
tendido *m adj* = lying (down), 29

tenemos = we have (See *tener*), 16
tenemos que = we have to; we must
    (See *tener que*), 24
tener = to have, 3
tener ganas de = to feel like, 18
tener la impresión de que = to have
    the impression that, 32
tener que = to have to; must, 23
tener razón = to be right, 17
tengo = I have (See *tener*), 2
tengo ganas de = I feel like (See *tener
    ganas de*), 18
tengo miedo = I am afraid, 2
terremoto *m* = earthquake, 28
terrible *m,f adj* = dreadful; terrible, 22
ti = you (*s, familiar*) (After a
    preposition), 31
tibio *f adj* = warm, 34
tiemblo = I tremble (See *temblar*), 5
tiempo *m* = time; weather, 27
tienes razón = you (*s, familiar*) are
    right (See *tener razón*), 17
tierra *f* = earth, 28
tipo *m* = type; sort, 19
tocamos = we touch (See *tocar*), 16
tocar = to touch; to knock, 16
todavía = still; yet, 30
todo = all; everything, 27
todos los días = every day, 1
tomar = to take, 28
tomo = I take (See *tomar*), 20
tonta *f adj* = foolish; silly, 32
toquemos = let's touch (See *tocar*), 16
tormenta *f* = (thunder)storm, 24
tormentoso *m adj* = stormy, 29
tragar saliva = to swallow hard;
    to gulp, 26
tranquilizar = to put someone's mind
    at ease, 32
tranquilizarse = to calm down, 11
trasero *m* = derriere, 13
tratar de = to try to, 16
través de (a) = through; across, 44
tres = three, 3
treta *f* = trick; ruse, 32
tristeza *f* = sadness, 23
trompo *m* = spinning top, 23

tronar = to thunder, 44
truco *m* = trick, 29
trueno *m* = clap of thunder;
    thunderclap, 24
truenos *m, pl* = thunder, 24
tu *m,f adj* = your, 18
tú *s, familiar* = you, 1
¿tú estás bien? = are you O.K.?, 34
tumba *f* = tomb, 19

última *f adj* = last, 12
umbral *m* = threshold, 44
umbral de la puerta = door's
    threshold; doorway, 33
un *m* = a, 7
una *f* = a, 7
única *f adj* = only, 14
uno *m adj* = one, 3
usted *s, polite* = you, 1
ustedes *pl* = you, 1

vacía *f adj* = empty, 13
vacío *m adj* = empty, 33
valiente *m,f adj* = courageous;
    brave, 18
valor *m* = bravery; courage, 22
vamos = we are going (See *ir*), 22
vamos a = we are going to, 12
vas = you (*s, familiar*) are going
    (See *ir*), 6
¡vaya! = well! (See *ir*), 36
veces *f, pl* = times (See *vez*), 3
velocidad *f* = speed, 21

vemos = we see (See *ver*), 12
venir = to come, 44
veo = I see (See *ver*), 9
ver = to see; to witness, 17
verdad *f* = truth, 28
verdaderamente = really, 32
verdadero *m adj* = true; real, 22
verde *m,f adj* = green, 14
vergüenza *f* = shame;
    embarrassment, 46
vestido *m* = dress, 14
vestido *m adj* = dressed, 14
vez *f* = time, 26
vez (a su) = in turn, 30
vida *f* = life, 26
vieja *f* = old; old lady, 11
viejo *m* = old; old man, 11
viento *m* = wind, 18
vientos huracanados = gale force
    winds, 25
vista *f* = sight; eyes, 8
viva *f adj* = alive, 14
volverse = to turn, 21
voz *f* = voice, 5
vuelta *f* = turn, 33
vuelta (darse la) = to turn around, 33

y = and, 2
ya = already, 29
ya no = no longer; not any more, 22
yo = I, 1
yo también = me too, 13
yo tampoco = me neither, 12

~~ ABOUT THE AUTHOR ~~

The author is an Indiana University graduate and former medical doctor educated at the Université de Paris, France. She also attended the Sorbonne in Paris and received a Certificat de Phonétique Appliquée à la Langue Française. Having lived and worked in Paris for 13 years, she now has dual nationality. She has most recently become a writer and teacher, using her life experiences in the creation of *The Twisted Doors* series. Dr. Dior is currently using *Les portes tordues* to teach French at the Purdue University Gifted Education Resource Institute in West Lafayette, Indiana.